THE SCIENCE AND SPIRIT OF RESILIENCE

EXPLORING THE INTERSECTION OF NEUROSCIENCE, PSYCHOLOGY, AND SPIRITUAL WISDOM

ELLIOTT MIDDLETON PHD

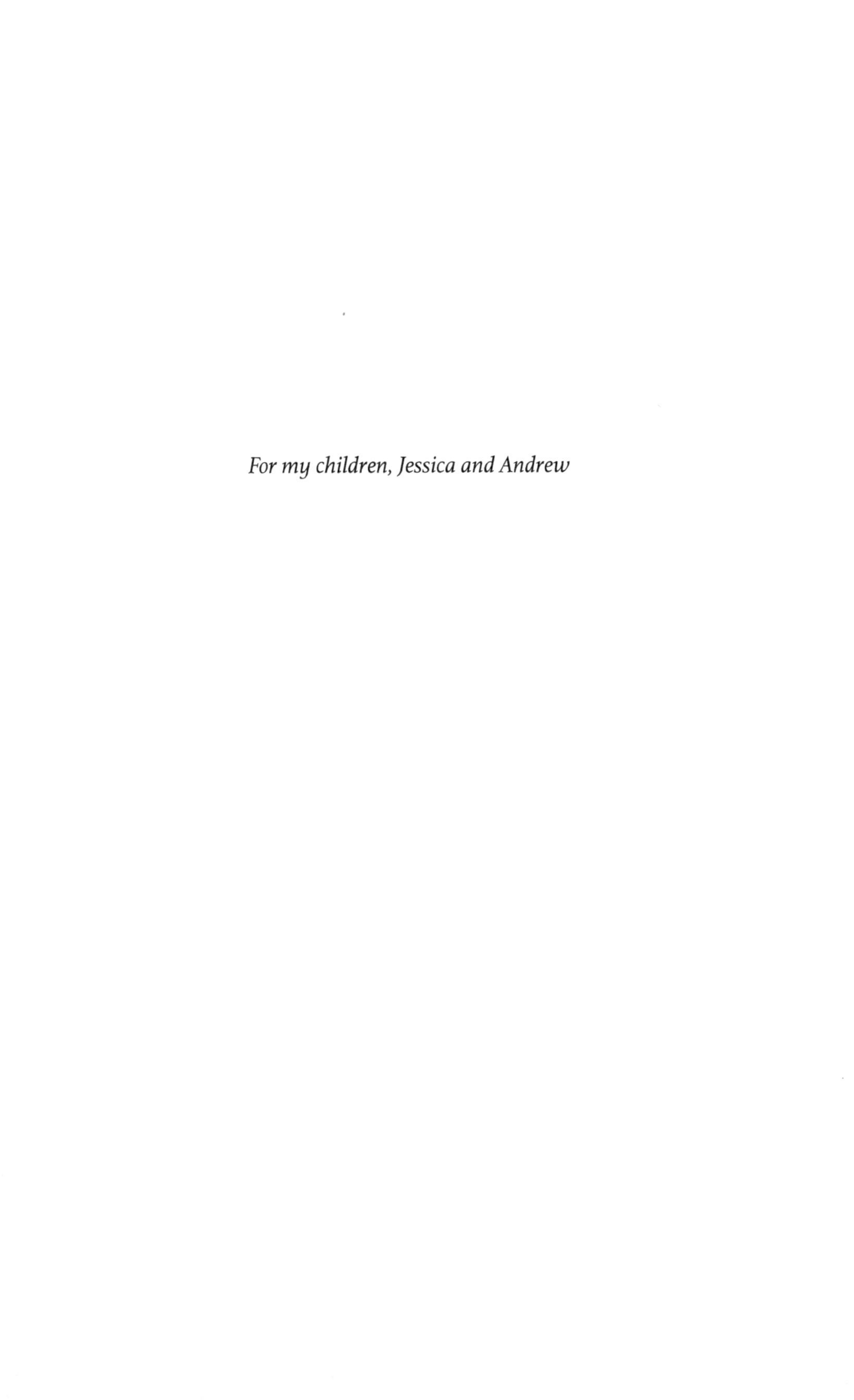

For my children, Jessica and Andrew

The oak fought the wind and was broken, the willow bent when it must and survived.

— ROBERT JORDAN

INTRODUCTION

Resilience, as we will come to understand, is not just a survival tool but a transformative force. It is best grasped not through abstract theories but through the real lives of those who have faced the flames of adversity and emerged stronger. Consider the story of Nelson Mandela, a beacon of resilience, who, after 27 years of imprisonment under the oppressive apartheid regime, didn't just survive but led South Africa out of decades of racial division. His journey is a testament to the transformative power of resilience, the ability to maintain hope, adapt, and ultimately transform not only his own life but the fate of a nation. Through stories like these, we can truly understand the essence of resilience: the capacity to withstand, adapt to, and grow from life's trials.

At its core, resilience is the ability to thrive in adversity. It is not merely surviving difficult circumstances but finding ways to grow and flourish despite them. Every person faces emotional, physical, social, or spiritual challenges, and their resilience determines whether those challenges become overwhelming burdens or catalysts for growth. Whether dealing with personal loss, professional setbacks, or unexpected crises, resilience empowers individuals to recover and emerge more robust and capable.

This book is about understanding resilience and equipping you with practical tools to build it in your own life. It combines scientific research and Biblical teachings to guide you toward creating the strength necessary to navigate life's challenges. We will explore what neuroscience reveals about the human brain's ability to adapt and rewire itself in the face of hardship, offering practical tools for personal growth. At the same time, we will turn to timeless Biblical examples, where resilience is woven into the fabric of many stories. These two perspectives—one grounded in cutting-edge science and the other in spiritual wisdom—will combine to offer a comprehensive guide to becoming more resilient.

This book is not a quick fix but a comprehensive guide for those seeking to develop deep, lasting resilience. It is tailored to those who want to build an innate, lasting ability to overcome obstacles, whether in personal trials, work pressures, or spiritual challenges. This book will speak to those seeking a balance between intellectual understanding and faith-driven insights by engaging scientific evidence and spiritual reflection. It's a journey, not a sprint; we're in it together, covering all aspects of resilience.

What sets this book apart is its unique approach. We will delve into the latest findings in neuroscience, such as the concept of neuroplasticity, which demonstrates the brain's ability to change and adapt. These scientific insights will be paired with Biblical teachings that offer spiritual and emotional resilience. This combination will provide you with a holistic understanding of resilience that integrates the mind, body, and spirit.

The structure of the book follows a logical progression. Chapter 1 delves into the **neuroscience of resilience**, explaining how the brain responds to stress and adapts through mechanisms like neuroplasticity. Chapter 2 focuses on **emotional resilience**, discussing how emotional regulation is critical to overcoming adversity. In Chapter 3, we will explore the **role of neuroplasticity** in building resilience and how you can cultivate it in your life. Chapter 4 covers the **psychology of coping mechanisms**, while Chapter 5 introduces the importance of **emotional intelligence** in resilience. Chapter 6 addresses **social and environmental factors,** helping you understand how relationships and surroundings influence your ability to bounce back from adversity. Chapter 7 offers **practical stress-management techniques** you can use daily, and finally, Chapter 8 will show you how to build a robust **support system** that bolsters your resilience.

Before we dive deeper, I want to share a personal experience with resilience. Like many of you, I have faced moments of intense challenge, moments when it seemed easier to give up than to keep pushing forward. One particular hardship stands out in my memory: I faced professional failure that threatened my career and my sense of identity and purpose. During this period, I turned to the practical strategies I had learned—such as Mindfulness and emotional regulation—and the wisdom of Scripture, drawing strength from the stories of perseverance and faith. Through this, I knew that resilience is not built in moments of ease but through the fire of adversity. In many ways, this book is a product of that experience, and I hope it will provide you with the tools to face your challenges with renewed strength and hope.

Expect practical takeaways from this book that will help you cultivate resilience in every area of your life. You will gain insights into how to rewire your brain for resilience, manage your emotions during difficult times, and build strong, supportive relationships. Each chapter contains actionable strategies grounded in scientific research and Biblical wisdom that you can implement immediately. Whether through mindful breathing, reframing negative thoughts, or learning from Biblical figures like Job and Joseph, this book offers a practical roadmap to resilience, empowering you with the tools you need to face life's challenges.

Let this book be your companion on the journey toward becoming a more resilient person. No matter what difficulties you face, know that resilience is not an inherent trait but a skill that can be developed. You can overcome challenges, grow stronger with each obstacle, and find meaning even in hardship. As we move through the pages of this book, may you be inspired, equipped, and empowered to embrace the strength within you, guided by our unique approach that integrates scientific research and Biblical wisdom.

1

UNDERSTANDING THE FOUNDATIONS OF RESILIENCE

Resilience is not something people are born with; it's a capacity that can be cultivated, developed, and refined over time, mainly through adversity. The brain is at the heart of this process, a remarkable organ that can reorganize and learn from challenging experiences. To understand how we can become more resilient, it is essential first to explore how the brain processes stress and adversity and how it can grow stronger in these challenges.

The Neuroscience of Resilience

When stress or adversity strikes, the brain springs into action with a series of intricate responses. At the forefront of this reaction is the amygdala, a small, almond-shaped region nestled deep within the brain. This crucial component, often referred to as the brain's alarm system, is responsible for detecting potential threats, whether real or perceived. It then sets off the body's 'fight or flight' response, releasing stress hormones like cortisol and adrenaline. These hormones prepare the body to confront or escape the danger as needed (LeDoux, 2000).

Resilience is not about eliminating stress, as stress is a natural and sometimes necessary part of life. What sets resilient individuals apart is their ability to regulate their emotional responses to stress. This is where the prefrontal cortex, located at the front of the brain, comes into play. Responsible for higher-order functions like decision-making, impulse control, and emotional regulation, a well-functioning prefrontal cortex can help mitigate the amygdala's stress response. It allows us to assess the situation calmly and make rational decisions rather than reacting impulsively out of fear (Arnsten, 2009).

However, prolonged stress can take a toll on the prefrontal cortex, making it harder to regulate emotions and respond thoughtfully to adversity. In such situations, individuals might experience heightened anxiety, difficulty concentrating, or even a sense of helplessness. It's crucial to strengthen the prefrontal cortex's ability to manage stress, which can be done through targeted practices like Mindfulness and cognitive-behavioral techniques, as we'll explore later in this chapter.

Neurotransmitters, the brain's chemical messengers, also play an essential role in how we experience and manage stress. **Serotonin** and **dopamine**, in particular, are critical in regulating mood and motivation. Serotonin, often called the "feel-good" neurotransmitter, contributes to feelings of well-being and happiness. Low levels of serotonin have been linked to depression and anxiety, making it more challenging to bounce back from setbacks. Dopamine, on the other hand, is involved in reward-seeking and motivation. It drives us to pursue goals and persevere through difficult circumstances (Krishnan & Nestler, 2008). The delicate balance of these neurotransmitters directly impacts our ability to maintain emotional stability in the face of stress.

Neuroplasticity: The Brain's Ability to Adapt

One of the most exciting discoveries in neuroscience is the concept of **neuroplasticity**, which refers to the brain's remarkable ability to reorganize itself by forming new neural connections. This adaptability is a beacon of hope for resilience, as it allows the brain to recover from stress and trauma, learn from experience, and become more efficient in handling future challenges. Neuroplasticity makes the brain malleable, meaning it can change and improve over time, much like a stronger muscle with repeated use.

A fascinating example of neuroplasticity can be found in the brains of **London taxi drivers**. These drivers must memorize an intricate mental map of London's streets—a feat known as "The Knowledge." Studies have shown that taxi drivers have a significantly larger **hippocampus**—the part of the brain responsible for memory and spatial navigation—than non-taxi drivers. This structural difference illustrates how the brain can physically change in response to learning and experience (Maguire et al., 2000). The lesson here is that the brain can adapt to new challenges, and this adaptability is a critical component of resilience.

Practices like **Mindfulness** and **meditation** are powerful tools that promote neuroplasticity, particularly in brain areas involved in emotional regulation. Research has demonstrated that regular Mindfulness practice can increase the thickness of the prefrontal cortex while reducing the size of the amygdala. These changes correspond to improved emotional control and reduced stress reactivity (Davidson & Kabat-Zinn, 2003). By engaging in Mindfulness, individuals can actively rewire their brains to become more resilient, improving their capacity to handle adversity and taking control of their mental well-being.

Scientific Studies on Brain Plasticity and Resilience

A growing body of research supports the idea that the brain's capacity for neuroplasticity is integral to resilience. **Longitudinal studies** tracking individuals over time show that the brain can change in response to chronic stress but can also recover when stress is effectively managed. For example, individuals exposed to prolonged caregiving responsibilities—such as those looking after a terminally ill relative—often show signs of **prefrontal cortex** atrophy due to chronic stress. However, when these individuals engage in **stress-reduction techniques** like Mindfulness or cognitive-behavioral therapy (CBT), their brains can recover, regaining structure and function (McEwen, 2007).

One study led by Holzel et al. (2011) found that individuals who participated in an eight-week Mindfulness meditation program experienced increased gray matter density in regions of the brain associated with memory, emotional regulation, and self-awareness. The brain's plasticity allows it to grow stronger in response to practices that promote resilience.

Another study by Davidson et al. (2003) showed that participants who engaged in Mindfulness meditation had lower cortisol levels, the primary stress hormone, after only a few weeks of practice. This reduction in cortisol was accompanied by changes in brain activity, particularly in areas associated with emotional regulation and stress response. These findings highlight the direct link between neuroplasticity and the development of resilience.

Practical Applications for Building Resilience

Understanding the brain's role in resilience opens up many strategies for strengthening your ability to cope with stress. Below are several evidence-based techniques that can help you enhance your resilience:

- **Brain Training Exercises:** Activities that challenge the brain—such as learning a new language, playing strategy games, or solving puzzles—can stimulate neuroplasticity. These exercises improve cognitive flexibility, problem-solving skills, and emotional regulation, contributing to resilience. Regularly engaging in intellectually stimulating tasks helps to build a brain better equipped to handle adversity.

- **Mindfulness and Meditation:** Mindfulness practices reduce stress and promote brain changes that enhance resilience. By focusing on the present moment and observing thoughts and emotions without judgment, you can improve emotional regulation and prevent stress from overwhelming you. Simple Mindfulness techniques, such as mindful breathing or body scans, can be incorporated into your daily routine to cultivate a more resilient mindset.

- **Physical Activity:** Exercise is not only beneficial for the body but also for the brain. Aerobic activities like running, swimming, or cycling stimulate the production of **brain-derived neurotrophic factor (BDNF)**, a protein that promotes the growth of new neurons and strengthens existing neural connections. Physical activity increases neurogenesis, particularly in the **hippocampus**, essential for memory and emotional resilience (Erickson et al., 2011).

- **Healthy Nutrition:** A balanced diet rich in nutrients that support brain function is essential for resilience. Foods high in **omega-3 fatty acids**, such as salmon and flaxseeds, promote brain health by reducing inflammation and supporting neurotransmitter function. **Antioxidants** in fruits and vegetables protect the brain from oxidative stress, while **proteins** help regulate energy levels and mood. By nourishing the brain with the proper nutrients, you can enhance its ability to cope with stress (Gomez-Pinilla, 2008).

Emotional Resilience: Why It Matters

While cognitive resilience is vital, **emotional resilience**—the ability to recover from emotional challenges and maintain emotional balance—is equally crucial. Emotional resilience allows individuals to process negative emotions without becoming overwhelmed by them. It is the foundation for maintaining well-being in the face of adversity and enables us to continue functioning effectively in our personal and professional lives.

Emotional resilience differs from general resilience because it focuses on managing our emotional responses. People with high emotional resilience are likelier to maintain a positive outlook even during tough times and recover more quickly from emotional setbacks. This resilience helps protect against long-term mental health issues such as depression and anxiety (Bonanno, 2004).

A core aspect of emotional resilience is **emotional regulation**—the ability to manage and modulate emotions in response to stressful events. Techniques like **cognitive reappraisal**, which involves reframing negative thoughts in a more positive or neutral light, can help reduce the emotional impact of stressful situations. By changing the way you think about a problem, you can change how you feel about it, which helps build resilience. Emotional regulation also plays a vital role in relationships, enabling individuals to handle conflicts and challenges without damaging their interpersonal connections (Gross & John, 2003).

Biblical Example: Joseph's Perseverance Through Faith

Joseph's story is one of the Bible's most potent examples of resilience. As detailed in Genesis 37-50, Joseph's life was marked by extreme adversity, beginning with his brothers selling him into slavery. Despite this betrayal, Joseph exhibited remarkable resilience, adapting to each challenge with faith and perseverance. His journey from an enslaved person to a powerful leader in Egypt illustrates how resilience is about surviving adversity and thriving in its midst.

Joseph's story exemplifies **emotional resilience**. After being sold into slavery, the men his brothers sold him to took him to Egypt and sold him again into the household of an Egyptian official named Potiphar. Even when falsely accused by Potiphar's wife of harassing her and imprisoned unjustly, Joseph maintained his faith and integrity. He did not allow bitterness or despair to consume him, choosing instead to remain steadfast in his trust in God's plan. In prison, Joseph used his gifts to interpret the dreams of his fellow inmates, which eventually led to his release and rise to prominence as Pharaoh's second-in-command (Genesis 41:39-41).

What stands out in Joseph's story is his ability to adapt to each setback without losing sight of his ultimate purpose. His resilience was not a passive acceptance of suffering but an active engagement with his circumstances, always seeking to serve God and others no matter the situation. Joseph's emotional resilience allowed him to forgive his brothers, who had betrayed him, and use his power to save the people of Egypt and his family during a severe famine (Genesis 45:4-5).

In many ways, Joseph's journey mirrors the concept of **neuroplasticity**. Joseph's faith and character grew through each trial as the brain can reorganize and grow stronger in response to challenges. His ability to forgive and act gracefully after enduring such hardships illustrates a higher form of resilience rooted in emotional strength, faith, and a sense of divine purpose.

Joseph's life offers us a powerful example of how resilience is more than just enduring hardships. It is about transformation—allowing adversity to shape and strengthen us so that we emerge unchanged and better. His resilience resulted from his practical wisdom in managing Egypt's resources during the famine and reflected his deep trust in God. His ability to look beyond immediate circumstances and trust in a more fantastic plan is a timeless reminder that resilience involves maintaining perspective and faith, even when the road is uncertain.

R EFERENCES

Arnsten, A. F. (2009). Stress signaling pathways impair prefrontal cortex structure and function. *Nature Reviews Neuroscience, 10*(6), 410-422.

Bonanno, G. A. (2004). Loss, trauma, and human resilience: Have we underestimated the human capacity to thrive after extremely aversive events? *American Psychologist, 59*(1), 20–28.

Davidson, R. J., & Kabat-Zinn, J. (2003). Alterations in brain and immune function produced by Mindfulness meditation. *Psychosomatic Medicine, 65*(4), 564-570.

Erickson, K. I., Voss, M. W., Prakash, R. S., Basak, C., Szabo, A., Chaddock, L., & Kramer, A. F. (2011). Exercise training increases size of hippocampus and improves memory. *Proceedings of the National Academy of Sciences, 108*(7), 3017-3022.

Gomez-Pinilla, F. (2008). Brain foods: The effects of nutrients on brain function. *Nature Reviews Neuroscience, 9*(7), 568-578.

Gross, J. J., & John, O. P. (2003). Individual differences in two emotion regulation processes: Implications for affect, relationships, and well-being. *Journal of Personality and Social Psychology, 85*(2), 348-362.

Holzel, B. K., Carmody, J., Vangel, M., Congleton, C., Yerramsetti, S. M., Gard, T., & Lazar, S. W. (2011). Mindfulness practice leads to increases in regional brain gray matter density. *Psychiatry Research: Neuroimaging, 191*(1), 36-43.

Krishnan, V., & Nestler, E. J. (2008). The molecular neurobiology of depression. *Nature, 455*(7215), 894-902.

LeDoux, J. E. (2000). Emotion circuits in the brain. *Annual Review of Neuroscience, 23*, 155-184.

Maguire, E. A., Gadian, D. G., Johnsrude, I. S., Good, C. D., Ashburner, J., Frackowiak, R. S., & Frith, C. D. (2000). Navigation-related structural change in the hippocampi of taxi drivers. *Proceedings of the National Academy of Sciences, 97*(8), 4398-4403.

McEwen, B. S. (2007). Physiology and neurobiology of stress and adaptation: Central role of the brain. *Physiological Reviews, 87*(3), 873-904.

2

PRACTICAL TECHNIQUES FOR DAILY STRESS MANAGEMENT

Daily stress is an inevitable part of modern life. Stress can accumulate and undermine your well-being, whether facing a tight work deadline, balancing family life demands, or dealing with unexpected events. While some levels of stress can be motivating, chronic or unmanaged stress can have detrimental effects on both physical and mental health. Fortunately, science and experience provide us with various tools that can help mitigate stress and enhance resilience. This chapter will explore several practical techniques for managing daily stress, focusing on Mindfulness, deep breathing, time management, cognitive-behavioral strategies, sleep, and nutrition. Each method is backed by scientific research and offers actionable steps to help you cultivate calm and balance in your life.

Mindfulness Exercises for Stress Reduction

For good reason, Mindfulness has become a cornerstone of modern stress management. Mindfulness, at its core, is the practice of paying attention to the present moment and fully accepting it without judgment. It involves being fully aware of what you are doing and where you are, without being overly reactive or overwhelmed by what's happening around you. While the concept is simple, its effects on the brain and body can be profound. By cultivating a mindful approach to life, we can learn to observe our thoughts and emotions without becoming overwhelmed.

Mindfulness is particularly effective in reducing stress because it interrupts the habitual patterns of worry and rumination that often fuel anxiety. By focusing on the present moment, Mindfulness allows us to break free from the mental loops of what might happen in the future or what went wrong in the past, both familiar sources of stress. Instead, it anchors us in the here and now, creating a space for calm and clarity (Hofmann et al., 2010).

Mindfulness Meditation Techniques

Several Mindfulness meditation techniques, which are simple and easy to incorporate into daily life, can help reduce stress and promote emotional resilience. These techniques are not complex or time-consuming, making them accessible to everyone.

- **Body Scan Meditation:** This technique involves mentally scanning your body from head to toe, bringing awareness to each part without judgment. As you progress through each area of your body, notice any tension or discomfort and consciously relax those muscles. The body scan helps increase awareness of physical sensations and encourages relaxation, making it a powerful tool for releasing stress stored in the body.

- **Loving-Kindness Meditation:** This practice focuses on cultivating compassion and kindness toward yourself and others. It involves silently repeating phrases like, "May I be happy, may I be healthy, may I be at peace," and extending the exact wishes to others. This form of meditation promotes emotional well-being and fosters empathy and connection, reducing feelings of loneliness and stress.

- **Guided Imagery:** In this practice, you mentally visualize a peaceful or calming scene, such as a beach or forest, immersing yourself in the sensory details of the environment. Guided imagery helps to evoke a state of relaxation. It can be advantageous when dealing with high stress levels, as it transports the mind to a serene place, providing temporary relief from external pressures.

Daily Mindfulness Practices

In addition to formal meditation practices, there are several ways to bring Mindfulness into everyday activities. These techniques can be adapted to fit into your daily routine, making stress management a part of your everyday life.

- **Mindful Eating** involves eating slowly and deliberately, paying attention to each bite's taste, texture, and aroma. You can also practice Mindfulness while doing household chores, such as washing dishes or folding laundry, by focusing on the sensory experience and the movements of your body. Mindful eating enhances the enjoyment of food, helps prevent overeating, and improves digestion.

- **Mindful Walking:** While walking, focus on the sensation of your feet touching the ground, the rhythm of your breath, and the movement of your body. Mindful walking can transform an ordinary walk into a meditative experience, promoting physical and mental relaxation.

- **Mindful Breathing:** Taking a few minutes to focus solely on your breath can profoundly reduce stress. Observe the sensation of each inhalation and exhalation, allowing thoughts to come and go without attachment. This practice can be done anywhere, making it a versatile tool for stress management.

Scientific Evidence for Mindfulness

A growing body of scientific research supports the benefits of Mindfulness. Studies have shown that regular Mindfulness practice can significantly reduce cortisol levels, the body's primary stress hormone. For example, a study conducted by Carlson et al. (2007) found that participants in a Mindfulness-based stress reduction program experienced significant reductions in cortisol levels and improved mood and quality of life.

Furthermore, Mindfulness improves **emotional regulation**, enhances **mental clarity**, and increases **cognitive flexibility**, all of which are critical components of resilience (Hölzel et al., 2011). Psychological and biological changes occur as Mindfulness practice changes brain structure, particularly in areas controlling emotional regulation and self-awareness.

Deep Breathing Techniques for Instant Calm

Deep breathing is one of the simplest and most effective techniques for managing stress. When we experience stress, our body's **sympathetic nervous system** activates the fight-or-flight response, causing an increase in heart rate, blood pressure, and breathing rate. Deep breathing counteracts this by activating the **parasympathetic nervous system**, which promotes relaxation and helps restore balance to the body (Jerath et al., 2006).

Deep breathing works by increasing oxygen intake, which helps calm the brain and reduces the physiological symptoms of stress. By consciously slowing your breath, you can signal to your brain that you are safe, lowering cortisol levels and reducing the intensity of the stress response.

Breathing Exercises

Here are a few deep breathing techniques that can quickly calm the mind and body:

- **Diaphragmatic Breathing:** Also known as belly breathing, this technique involves breathing deeply into the diaphragm rather than shallowly into the chest. To practice diaphragmatic breathing, place one hand on your chest and the other on your abdomen. Breathe in slowly through your nose, allowing your abdomen to rise as you fill your lungs with air. Then, exhale slowly through your mouth. This type of breathing engages the diaphragm, promoting relaxation and reducing stress.

- **4-7-8 Breathing Method:** This technique, developed by Dr. Andrew Weil, is handy for calming anxiety and preparing for sleep. It involves inhaling through your nose for a count of 4, holding your breath for a count of 7, and then exhaling completely through your mouth for a count of 8. Repeat the cycle several times. The extended exhale helps activate the parasympathetic nervous system, promoting a sense of calm.

- **Box Breathing:** Commonly used by Navy SEALs to maintain focus and calm in high-pressure situations, box breathing involves inhaling for 4 seconds, holding your breath for 4 seconds, exhaling for 4 seconds, and holding your breath again for 4 seconds. This method helps regulate breathing and provides an immediate sense of control over stress.

Situational Applications for Deep Breathing

Deep breathing techniques can be applied in a variety of situations to provide immediate relief from stress. Whether it's before a stressful meeting or during moments of anxiety, these techniques can help you regain control and reduce the intensity of your stress.

- **Before a Stressful Meeting or Presentation:** Practicing diaphragmatic breathing or the 4-7-8 method can help calm nerves and improve focus before entering a high-stress situation.

- **During Moments of Anxiety or Panic:** If you feel anxiety rising, using box breathing can help you regain control of your breath and reduce the physical symptoms of panic.

- **As a Daily Relaxation Practice:** Incorporating a few minutes of deep breathing into your daily routine can lower baseline stress levels and improve overall well-being.

Benefits of Regular Practice

In addition to immediate stress relief, regular deep breathing practice offers long-term benefits, including:

- **Improved Focus and Concentration:** Deep breathing enhances cognitive function by increasing oxygen flow to the brain and helps improve attention and decision-making.

- **Enhanced Emotional Stability:** Deep breathing reduces the body's physiological response to stress, helping maintain emotional balance in difficult situations.

Time Management Tips for a Balanced Life

Effective time management is a crucial component of stress management. When we feel overwhelmed by tasks and responsibilities, stress can build up and lead to burnout. Organizing your time and setting clear priorities can prevent stress from accumulating and maintain control over your day.

Good time management involves more than just checking items off a to-do list. It requires thoughtful planning and a focus on balancing work, family, and self-care. Managing time adroitly reduces the mental load, leaving more room for relaxation and recovery.

Time Management Techniques

Here are several techniques that can help you manage your time more efficiently:

- **Eisenhower Matrix:** This method helps you prioritize tasks based on urgency and importance. You can focus your energy on what truly matters by categorizing tasks into four quadrants—urgent and important, important but not urgent, urgent but not important, and neither urgent nor important.

- **Time Blocking and Scheduling:** Allocate specific time slots for each task throughout the day. Tools like Google Calendar or time-blocking planners can help you organize your tasks and ensure that you stay on track. Scheduling time for breaks and relaxation is just as important as scheduling work tasks.

- **The Pomodoro Technique:** This popular time management technique involves working in focused intervals of 25 minutes, followed by a 5-minute break.

After four cycles, take a longer break of 15-30 minutes. The Pomodoro Technique helps maintain focus and prevents burnout by encouraging regular breaks.

Tools and Apps for Time Management

Several tools and apps can assist with time management, making it easier to stay organized and reduce stress:

- **Trello or Asana:** These apps allow you to organize tasks and projects visually, making it easy to track progress and collaborate.

- **Google Calendar:** Use Google Calendar to schedule tasks, appointments, and breaks, ensuring that you have a clear plan for your day.

- **Focus@Will:** This app provides scientifically designed background music to enhance focus and productivity, helping you maintain concentration during work sessions.

Personal Case Studies: Time Management in Action

- **A Working Parent Balancing Job and Family:** Consider the example of a working parent who struggles to balance their professional responsibilities with family obligations. By implementing time blocking, they designate specific hours for work, family time, and personal relaxation. They use apps like Google Calendar to schedule work meetings and family activities, ensuring that neither aspect of their life is neglected. Over time, this structured approach reduces stress, improves productivity at work, and fosters stronger family relationships.

- **A Student Managing Academic and Social Life:** University students are often overwhelmed by their academic workload and social commitments. Using the Pomodoro Technique, they break down their study sessions into manageable chunks, allowing for brief social interactions and relaxation between study periods. This method helps them focus better and prevents burnout, enabling them to excel academically while maintaining a fulfilling social life.

Cognitive Behavioral Strategies for Stress Management

Cognitive Behavioral Therapy (CBT) is a widely used and highly effective approach for managing stress and anxiety. CBT operates on the premise that our thoughts, emotions, and behaviors are interconnected, and by altering negative thought patterns, we can change how we feel and act in stressful situations. CBT helps individuals identify and challenge unhelpful thought patterns, replacing them with more realistic and positive perspectives.

CBT Techniques

Here are a few CBT techniques to manage stress:

- **Cognitive Restructuring:** This technique involves identifying and reframing negative or distorted thoughts more rationally and rationally. For example, if you think, "I can't handle this," cognitive restructuring would encourage you to challenge that thought by considering evidence to the contrary, such as when you have successfully managed similar challenges.

- **Behavioral Activation:** When feeling stressed or overwhelmed, it's common to withdraw from activities or responsibilities, which can exacerbate negative emotions. Behavioral activation encourages individuals to engage in positive activities, even when not motivated. Individuals can break the cycle of inactivity and improve their mood by taking small steps, such as going for a walk or meeting a friend for coffee.

- **Exposure Therapy:** For individuals who experience stress related to specific fears or anxieties, exposure therapy involves gradually confronting those fears in a controlled and safe environment. By facing the source of stress incrementally, the individual reduces the fear's power over time, leading to greater emotional resilience.

Applying CBT in Daily Life

CBT techniques can be applied to everyday stressors. For instance, when you notice a negative thought such as "I'll never meet this deadline," you can practice cognitive restructuring by asking yourself whether this thought is accurate and helpful. Instead, you might replace it with an idea like, "I've met deadlines before, and I can manage this by breaking the task into smaller steps."

Similarly, if you find yourself avoiding a critical task due to stress or anxiety, using behavioral activation to take the first small step can help you overcome inertia. For example, if the task is writing a report, you might start by writing the introduction. Once you've begun, you'll find it easier to continue.

Scientific Support for CBT

Psychological research has well-documented CBT's effectiveness. Studies have consistently shown that CBT can reduce symptoms of stress, anxiety, and depression. A meta-analysis of CBT's effectiveness revealed that it significantly improves emotional regulation and coping mechanisms (Butler et al., 2006). CBT is one of the most effective strategies for enhancing resilience when stressed.

The Science of Sleep and Its Impact on Resilience

Sleep is critical in resilience, allowing the body and mind to recover and recharge. Poor sleep, on the other hand, exacerbates stress, impairs cognitive function, and reduces emotional regulation. Without adequate sleep, maintaining focus, managing emotions, and handling life's challenges becomes much more challenging.

Sleep Hygiene Practices

Good sleep hygiene improves sleep quality. Here are some actionable tips for getting better sleep:

- **Establish a Regular Sleep Schedule:** Go to bed and wake up at the same time every day, even on weekends. This consistency helps regulate your body's internal clock, making it easier to fall asleep and wake up feeling refreshed.

- **Create a Sleep-Conducive Environment:** Ensure your bedroom is dark, quiet, and cool. Use blackout curtains or a sleep mask to block out light, and consider using earplugs or a white noise machine to eliminate disruptive sounds.

- **Limit Screen Time Before Bed:** The blue light emitted by phones, tablets, and computers can interfere with melatonin production, the hormone that regulates sleep. Avoid screens for at least an hour before bed to let your body wind down naturally.

Common Sleep Disorders and Their Effects on Resilience

Sleep disorders, such as **insomnia, sleep apnea,** and **restless legs syndrome,** can have a profound impact on resilience. These conditions disrupt vital sleep processes, making coping with stress and maintaining emotional balance harder. For example, insomnia, characterized by difficulty falling asleep or staying asleep, is strongly linked to increased anxiety and depression. Similarly, sleep apnea, a condition in which breathing repeatedly stops and starts during sleep, can lead to chronic fatigue and cognitive impairments.

If you suspect you have a sleep disorder, it's essential to seek medical advice. Addressing sleep disorders improves overall health and enhances resilience by allowing the body and brain to recover correctly each night.

Research on Sleep and Resilience

Research has consistently shown that sleep is a crucial factor in resilience. A study by Palmer and Alfano (2017) found that individuals who get sufficient, high-quality sleep are better equipped to handle stress, maintain emotional regulation, and recover from adversity. In contrast, sleep deprivation heightens emotional reactivity, poor decision-making, and increased vulnerability to stress-related disorders (Walker, 2017). These findings underscore the importance of prioritizing sleep as part of a holistic approach to resilience.

Nutrition and Resilience: Eating for Mental Toughness

What we eat directly impacts how we feel and how well we cope with stress. A balanced diet rich in nutrients supports brain function, improves mood, and enhances resilience. In contrast, a poor diet high in processed foods and sugar can contribute to mood swings, fatigue, and increased susceptibility to stress.

Link Between Diet and Mental Health

The **gut-brain axis** is the connection between the digestive system and the brain. This connection is crucial to mental health, as the gut produces neurotransmitters like serotonin, which regulate mood. Nutrients such as **omega-3 fatty acids**, **antioxidants**, and **protein** are essential for supporting brain health and reducing inflammation, which can contribute to stress and emotional instability (Gomez-Pinilla, 2008).

Dietary Recommendations for Mental Resilience

- **Omega-3 Fatty Acids:** Found in fish like salmon and sardines, flaxseeds, walnuts, and chia seeds, omega-3s are essential for brain health. They reduce inflammation and support neurotransmitter function, which is crucial for emotional resilience.

- **Antioxidant-Rich Fruits and Vegetables:** Berries, leafy greens, and other colorful fruits and vegetables provide antioxidants that protect the brain from oxidative stress, which can impair cognitive function and emotional stability.

- **Protein:** Lean proteins like chicken, tofu, and legumes help stabilize blood sugar levels, providing sustained energy and reducing mood fluctuations.

Meal Planning Tips

Planning and preparing balanced meals can make it easier to maintain a brain-healthy diet:

- **Simple, Nutritious Meal Prep:** Set aside time each week to prepare meals in advance, ensuring that you always have healthy options and reducing the temptation to reach for processed foods.

- **Balanced Meal Plate:** Aim to fill half your plate with vegetables, a quarter with lean protein, and a quarter with whole grains. This simple formula ensures a good mix of nutrients at each meal.

Scientific Evidence on Nutrition and Resilience

Research has shown that a diet rich in nutrients like omega-3 fatty acids, antioxidants, and vitamins is associated with better mental health outcomes. For example, Jacka et al. (2010) found that individuals who consumed a high-quality diet were less likely to experience depression and anxiety. Similarly, a study by Opie et al. (2015) demonstrated that whole-of-diet interventions, which emphasize nutrient-dense foods, can reduce symptoms of mental health disorders, including stress and depression.

Biblical Example: Jesus Calming the Storm

A powerful Biblical example of stress management and resilience can be found in the story of **Jesus calming the storm** (Mark 4:35-41). In this account, Jesus and His disciples were crossing the Sea of Galilee when a violent storm arose, threatening to capsize their boat. While the disciples panicked, fearing for their lives, Jesus remained calm, sleeping peacefully despite the chaos around Him. When the disciples woke Him, pleading for help, Jesus stood and rebuked the wind and waves, saying, "Peace! Be still!" Instantly, the storm ceased, and the sea became calm.

This story offers a profound lesson in resilience and emotional regulation. Despite being in a situation that would naturally induce fear and anxiety, Jesus maintained His inner calm, demonstrating the power of faith and trust in the face of adversity. His response to the storm serves as a model for how we can approach life's challenges. Rather than succumbing to panic or fear, we can cultivate inner peace and trust that we remain in control of our emotions even in the most chaotic circumstances.

For the disciples, the storm represented an external stressor they could not control. Their immediate reaction was fear and helplessness, much like how we often respond to the overwhelming challenges in our lives. But Jesus, through His unwavering calm, shows us that it is possible to remain composed and grounded, even during life's storms. His ability to quiet the storm with just a word symbolizes the inner peace we can cultivate through faith, Mindfulness, and trust in a higher power.

The story of **Jesus calming the storm** highlights several critical aspects of resilience:

1 **Emotional Regulation:** Jesus's ability to remain calm under extreme circumstances is a powerful example of emotional regulation. He did not react with fear or anxiety but responded with confi-

dence and peace. Similarly, when we face stress, we can learn to regulate our emotions through practices like Mindfulness and deep breathing, allowing us to respond to challenges more thoughtfully rather than reactively.

2 Faith as a Foundation for Resilience: Jesus's calm demeanor was rooted in His faith and trust in God's plan. For many, faith provides a solid foundation that enhances resilience. It offers a perspective that helps individuals rise above fear and uncertainty, knowing they are not alone in their struggles. Just as Jesus trusted in God's sovereignty over the storm, we, too, can place our trust in something greater than ourselves, which provides comfort and strength during difficult times.

3 Overcoming External Chaos with Internal Calm: The storm represents the chaos and unpredictability of life's external stressors. We often find ourselves in situations out of our control, much like the disciples on the boat. However, Jesus's response teaches us that while we may not always be able to control external events, we can control our internal state. By cultivating Mindfulness, emotional regulation, and faith, we develop the resilience to face life's storms with inner calm.

This story invites us to reflect on how we handle stress and adversity. Like the disciples, do we react with panic and fear when faced with challenges beyond our control? Or do we strive to emulate Jesus, cultivating an inner peace that allows us to navigate even the most turbulent situations with grace and composure? The story reminds us that true resilience is not the absence of storms but the ability to remain peaceful within them.

In our modern lives, we are often overwhelmed by the pace and pressure of daily responsibilities. Like the Sea of Galilee storm, these challenges can feel overwhelming and uncontrollable. Yet, by practicing the techniques outlined in this chapter—Mindfulness, deep breathing, time management, cognitive-behavioral strategies, sleep hygiene, and healthy nutrition—we can cultivate the emotional and physical resilience needed to face life's challenges confidently.

· · ·

REFERENCES

Butler, A. C., Chapman, J. E., Forman, E. M., & Beck, A. T. (2006). The empirical status of cognitive-behavioral therapy: A review of meta-analyses. *Clinical Psychology Review, 26*(1), 17-31.

Carlson, L. E., Speca, M., Patel, K. D., & Goodey, E. (2007). Mindfulness-based stress reduction in relation to quality of life, mood, symptoms of stress, and immune parameters in breast and prostate cancer outpatients. *Psychosomatic Medicine, 65*(4), 571-581.

Gomez-Pinilla, F. (2008). Brain foods: The effects of nutrients on brain function. *Nature Reviews Neuroscience, 9*(7), 568-578.

Hofmann, S. G., Sawyer, A. T., Witt, A. A., & Oh, D. (2010). The effect of Mindfulness-based therapy on anxiety and depression: A meta-analytic review. *Journal of Consulting and Clinical Psychology, 78*(2), 169-183.

Hölzel, B. K., Carmody, J., Evans, K. C., Hoge, E. A., Dusek, J. A., Morgan, L., ... & Lazar, S. W. (2011). Stress reduction correlates with structural changes in the amygdala. *Social Cognitive and Affective Neuroscience, 5*(1), 11-17.

Jacka, F. N., Kremer, P. J., Berk, M., De Silva-Sanigorski, A. M., Moodie, M., Leslie, E. R., ... & Swinburn, B. A. (2010). A prospective study of diet quality and mental health in adolescents. *PloS One, 5*(9), e24847.

Jerath, R., Edry, J. W., Barnes, V. A., & Jerath, V. (2006). Physiology of long pranayamic breathing: Neural respiratory elements may provide a mechanism that explains how slow deep breathing shifts the autonomic nervous system. *Medical Hypotheses, 67*(3), 566-571.

Opie, R. S., O'Neil, A., Itsiopoulos, C., & Jacka, F. N. (2015). The impact of whole-of-diet interventions on depression and anxiety: A systematic review of randomised controlled trials. *Public Health Nutrition, 18*(11), 2074-2093.

Palmer, C. A., & Alfano, C. A. (2017). Sleep and emotion regulation: An organizing, integrative review. *Sleep Medicine Reviews, 31*, 6-16.

Walker, M. (2017). *Why We Sleep: Unlocking the Power of Sleep and Dreams.* Scribner.

Mark 4:35-41 (New International Version).

3

BUILDING A STRONG SUPPORT SYSTEM

I solation does not breed resilience. A solid support system is one of the most critical components of resilience. Whether through personal relationships, professional networks, or community engagement, the people we surround ourselves with can provide the emotional, practical, and social resources needed to navigate life's challenges. This chapter explores building and sustaining meaningful connections that contribute to personal growth, emotional well-being, and long-term resilience.

Networking for Personal Growth

Networking, the process of making and using contacts for professional and personal growth, is often associated with career advancement. However, its benefits extend beyond job opportunities. A strong network exposes you to diverse perspectives, opens doors to new opportunities, and provides vital emotional and intellectual support. The relationships you form through networking can significantly contribute to your resilience by offering encouragement, mentorship, and practical advice when encountering obstacles.

- **Exposure to Diverse Perspectives and Ideas:** Networking introduces you to individuals with different experiences, worldviews, and skill sets. Engaging with various perspectives broadens your understanding of complex problems, helps you approach challenges creatively, and fosters a growth mindset. This exposure can inspire innovative solutions and give you the confidence to take risks in your personal and professional life (Granovetter, 1973).

- **Opportunities for Collaboration and Support:** Networking creates opportunities to collaborate with others on personal projects or professional ventures. Working with others allows you to pool resources, share knowledge, and tackle challenges together, which enhances your resilience by distributing the weight of adversity. Furthermore, knowing you have a network to rely on during difficult times can reduce feelings of isolation and helplessness.

Building a Network

Building a robust network requires intentional effort and a proactive approach. Whether you are seeking to grow professionally or enhance your personal life, there are several strategies you can employ to build meaningful connections:

- **Attending Industry Conferences and Events:** Conferences, seminars, and industry meetups are excellent opportunities to meet like-minded individuals and expand your professional network. Make a point to introduce yourself to others, exchange contact information, and follow up with new connections after the event.

- **Joining Professional Organizations or Clubs:** Professional groups and clubs related to your field of interest are valuable platforms for meeting individuals who share your goals and aspirations. These organizations often host regular events, workshops, and forums that provide networking opportunities and offer access to valuable resources.

Maintaining Connections

Building a network is just the beginning; maintaining those connections is equally important. Relationships require regular communication and nurturing to stay strong. The key to building a lasting network lies in staying connected, offering support, and showing genuine interest in the well-being of others.

- **Regular Check-ins and Follow-ups:** Stay in touch with your contacts by scheduling regular check-ins. A simple email, phone call, or text message can go a long way in maintaining relationships. Make it a habit to follow up after meetings or significant events to reinforce the connection.

Networking is not just about receiving support, but also about giving. Offer assistance when you can, whether by sharing resources, providing advice, or connecting people within your network. For instance, you can share a useful article with a colleague, offer to review a friend's resume, or introduce two people who could benefit from knowing each other. Being generous with your time and knowledge builds trust and strengthens relationships over the long term.

Leveraging Your Network

Once you have established a network, you must know how to leverage it effectively for personal and professional growth. Whether you need guidance, mentorship, or access to new opportunities, your network can serve as a valuable resource.

- **Seeking Advice and Mentorship:** Contact individuals in your network for advice or mentorship. Whether you are navigating a career transition or a personal challenge, having someone with experience to guide you can enhance your resilience by providing clarity and perspective.

- **Accessing New Opportunities Through Referrals:** Your network can connect you to new opportunities, such as job openings, collaborative projects, or learning experiences. When looking for new ways to grow, don't hesitate to ask for introductions or referrals from trusted contacts.

Fostering Deep Relationships

While professional networking is important, fostering deep, meaningful relationships is essential for emotional resilience. Emotional resilience is the ability to adapt to and cope with stressful situations or crises. These close relationships provide a sense of belonging, trust, and security vital for well-being, especially during adversity.

Deep relationships offer the emotional support needed to navigate life's most challenging moments, whether with friends, family, or a partner.

- **Emotional Support and Understanding**: Close relationships provide a safe space to share your fears, frustrations, and vulnerabilities without judgment. Emotional support from trusted individuals helps you process difficult emotions, reduces stress, and provides comfort during challenging times.

- **Increased Sense of Belonging and Security**: Having people you can rely on fosters a profound sense of belonging and emotional security. This feeling of connectedness is a protective factor against loneliness, anxiety, and depression. When you know you have a support system to fall back on, you are more likely to take risks and face challenges confidently, feeling reassured and safe.

Building Trust

Trust is the foundation of any strong relationship. Building trust requires time, effort, and consistent behavior that demonstrates reliability and transparency. Understanding your role in this process will make you feel empowered and self-assured.

- **Consistent Communication and Transparency**: Open and honest communication is critical to building trust in relationships. Be upfront about your thoughts, feelings, and expectations, and encourage others to do the same. By fostering an environment of transparency, you create a space where mutual trust can grow.

- **Keeping Promises and Demonstrating Reliability**: Actions build trust. When you commit, follow through. Reliability is one of the most essential factors in developing long-lasting relationships. When others know they can count on you, trust naturally deepens.

Strengthening Bonds

Deepening your relationships requires intentional effort and shared experiences. Investing time and energy into your closest relationships strengthens the bond between you and others, creating a more resilient and supportive network. Understanding the value of these shared experiences highlights the importance of investing in these connections.

- **Quality Time and Shared Activities:** Spending quality time together fosters close relationships. Engage in shared activities, such as cooking a meal together, going for a hike, or even just having a movie night, to deepen your connection with others. These experiences build a solid emotional foundation, making it easier to offer and receive support in times of need.

- **Open and Honest Communication:** Keep communication channels open by encouraging regular conversations about feelings, goals, and challenges. Being vulnerable and honest with loved ones fosters deeper emotional connections and allows both parties to better understand and support each other.

Conflict Resolution

Conflicts are inevitable in any relationship, but managing and resolving conflicts effectively is crucial for maintaining strong bonds. Conflict resolution skills help prevent misunderstandings and resentment from eroding relationships over time.

- **Active Listening and Empathy:** When conflicts arise, practice active listening. Focus on what the other person is saying without interrupting or forming a rebuttal in your mind. Empathy allows you to understand the other person's perspective, which is essential for resolving disputes amicably.

- **Compromise and Finding Common Ground:** Effective conflict resolution often involves compromise. Both parties can move forward without lingering resentment by finding common ground and making mutual concessions.

- **Apologizing and Forgiveness:** In any relationship, mistakes will happen. A sincere apology and willingness to forgive are essential for healing and moving forward after a conflict. Holding onto grudges can strain relationships, whereas forgiveness fosters emotional resilience and a stronger connection.

Building Community Support Systems

Beyond individual relationships, community support systems provide an additional layer of resilience. A strong community offers shared resources, collective problem-solving, and social support, vital for overcoming challenges and fostering personal growth.

• **Shared Resources and Information:** Communities provide access to collective knowledge, skills, and resources. Whether sharing information, offering practical assistance, or pooling financial resources, a supportive community helps its members navigate difficult situations more effectively.

• **Collective Problem-Solving and Support:** Communities can solve common problems by offering emotional and practical support. By working as a group, individuals benefit from the community's collective wisdom and resources, which enhances resilience for all members.

Engaging with Community

Becoming an active community member is a powerful way to build resilience and create a sense of belonging.

• **Volunteering for Local Organizations:** Volunteering is an excellent way to give back to your community while forming meaningful connections with others. It also fosters a sense of purpose and fulfillment, protective factors for mental health.

• **Participating in Community Events and Initiatives:** Engaging in local events, such as town hall meetings, social gatherings, or community improvement projects, helps you stay connected with those around you. Building a network of neighbors and peers strengthens your support system and makes you more resilient during times of crisis.

Creating Support Groups

Support groups are valuable spaces where individuals facing similar challenges can share their experiences, offer advice, and provide emotional support. These groups foster resilience by creating a network of individuals who understand and empathize with each other's struggles.

• **Identifying Common Needs and Interests:** When forming a support group, identify a shared need or interest among participants, such as a health condition, professional challenge, or personal goal.

• **Establishing Group Norms and Goals:** Set clear expectations for group meetings, including guidelines for confidentiality, participation, and communication. Establishing norms helps ensure the group remains a safe and supportive space for all members.

• **Scheduling Regular Meetings**: Consistency is critical to maintaining a solid support group. Schedule regular meetings to foster a sense of continuity and provide ongoing support.

Benefits of Community Support

The benefits of community support are vast, ranging from emotional and practical assistance to a greater sense of belonging.

Neighborhood Watch Programs: In many communities, neighborhood watch programs provide safety, security, and a shared sense of responsibility. These programs foster resilience by creating strong bonds among neighbors who look out for each other and share resources in times of need. By working together to keep the neighborhood safe, participants in these programs build trust, cooperation, and a sense of shared responsibility, enhancing the community's resilience.

• **Online Communities for Specific Interests or Challenges**: With the advent of the internet, individuals can now join virtual communities focused on specific interests or challenges. These online spaces provide an opportunity to connect with others facing similar experiences, whether coping with a chronic illness, pursuing a new career, or overcoming personal obstacles. These communities' collective wisdom and support can significantly bolster personal resilience, even if participants never meet face-to-face.

Leveraging Social Media for Emotional Support

In today's digital age, social media plays a significant role in connecting with others and building support networks. While it often gets criticized for fostering superficial connections, social media can be a valuable tool for emotional support when used mindfully.

• **Connecting with Like-Minded Individuals**: Social media platforms provide a space to connect with people with similar values, experiences, or interests. Whether through Facebook groups, Twitter communities, or specialized forums, individuals can find emotional support by engaging with others who understand their struggles. This sense of connection can be precious when geographical distance makes in-person support difficult.

- **Accessing Support Groups and Forums:** Online support groups are valuable for those seeking advice, encouragement, or simply a listening ear. These groups often focus on mental health, caregiving, or personal development, allowing participants to share their experiences and offer mutual support in a nonjudgmental environment. For many, these online communities provide a lifeline during times of crisis or isolation.

Building a Supportive Online Network

While social media has its pitfalls, it can be a powerful tool for building a positive and supportive network if used thoughtfully. Here are some tips for curating an online presence that enhances resilience:

- **Joining Relevant Groups and Communities:** Be intentional about the communities you engage with online. Seek out groups that align with your interests, goals, or values, and participate actively by sharing content, offering support, and engaging in discussions.

- **Sharing and Engaging with Uplifting Content:** Use your social media platforms to spread positivity and encouragement. Sharing uplifting articles, motivational quotes, or personal stories of resilience can foster a sense of connection and support among your online network.

Avoiding Negativity

While social media has the potential to foster positive connections, it can also become a source of stress if not managed carefully. Setting boundaries is essential for maintaining a healthy relationship with social media.

- **Setting Boundaries for Social Media Use:** Limit your time on social media to prevent being overwhelmed or burnt out. Consider setting daily time limits or designated periods during which you check your accounts. Limitations ensure that your online interactions are intentional rather than habitual.

• **Curating Your Feed to Avoid Toxic Content:** Be mindful of the content and people you follow on social media. If specific posts or interactions cause stress, anxiety, or frustration, consider muting or unfollowing those accounts. Curating a feed that reflects positivity and encouragement can significantly impact your mental and emotional well-being.

Real-Life Examples: Social Media for Emotional Support

• **Finding Support During a Health Crisis:** Consider the example of an individual facing a serious health diagnosis. By joining an online support group for people with the same condition, they can connect with others who understand their experience, share coping strategies, and provide emotional support. This sense of community helps reduce feelings of isolation and builds resilience during a challenging time.

• **Building a Community Around Shared Hobbies or Experiences:** Social media can also be a platform for building supportive communities around shared hobbies or experiences. For instance, someone who loves photography might join a group dedicated to this passion to share their work, receive constructive feedback, and connect with others who share their enthusiasm. These connections offer emotional support and foster resilience through creative expression.

The Role of Mentors in Building Resilience

Having a mentor can be a game-changer when it comes to building resilience. Mentors guide, encourage, and support you during uncertainty, helping you navigate challenges more confidently and clearly. A mentor's experience can offer valuable insights, and their belief in your abilities can bolster your self-esteem and sense of direction.

• **Guidance and Advice from Experienced Individuals:** Mentors draw from their experiences to offer practical advice and strategies for overcoming obstacles. Whether you face professional challenges, personal growth hurdles, or difficult life decisions, a mentor's guidance can help you find solutions and stay focused on your goals.

• **Emotional Support and Encouragement:** Beyond offering practical advice, mentors provide emotional support by believing in your potential and helping you maintain perspective. Their encouragement can be invaluable when self-doubt or uncertainty threatens your resilience.

Finding a Mentor

Finding a mentor requires a proactive approach. Whether you seek guidance in your career, personal life, or a specific skill set, you can take steps to identify and connect with potential mentors.

• **Seeking Mentors Within Your Industry or Community:** Look within your professional or personal network for individuals with the experience and insight to guide you. Attend networking events, workshops, or community gatherings to meet potential mentors and build relationships.

• **Crafting a Compelling Mentorship Request:** When approaching a potential mentor, be clear about what you seek and why you believe they are the right person to help you. A well-thought-out mentorship request should articulate your goals, the areas where you seek guidance, and how you value their expertise.

Maintaining the Mentorship Relationship

The key to a successful mentor-mentee relationship is regular communication and mutual respect. Mentorship is not a one-way street; it requires effort from both parties to be effective.

• **Regular, Scheduled Meetings:** Meet your mentor regularly to discuss progress, challenges, and new goals. These check-ins ensure that you and your mentor remain engaged in the relationship.

• **Setting Clear Goals and Expectations:** Clarify your expectations for the mentorship relationship from the outset. Whether seeking career advice, emotional support, or skill development, being clear about your goals helps your mentor tailor their guidance to your needs.

• **Showing Appreciation and Giving Feedback:** Be grateful for your mentor's time and advice. Feedback is also essential—let them know how their guidance has helped you grow or overcome challenges. This communication fosters a positive and productive relationship.

Benefits of Mentorship

The benefits of having a mentor extend beyond immediate problem-solving. Mentorship enhances long-term resilience by equipping you with the tools, confidence, and emotional support to face future challenges.

• **Career Advancement and Personal Growth**: A mentor's guidance can lead to significant career advancements, such as promotions, new opportunities, or skill development. Mentorship can also help you achieve personal growth by offering new perspectives on challenges and solutions.

• **Overcoming Specific Challenges with Mentor Guidance**: Consider the example of an entrepreneur struggling to navigate the complexities of running a business. A mentor who has successfully managed similar challenges can provide actionable advice, helping the mentee overcome obstacles with greater ease and resilience.

Family Dynamics and Resilience

Family is often our first and most important source of emotional and practical support. Strong family relationships can be decisive in building resilience, providing stability and security that helps individuals navigate life's most challenging moments.

• **Emotional and Practical Support During Crises**: During crises, family members often provide emotional and practical support, helping individuals cope with stress, loss, or uncertainty. Whether through financial assistance, caregiving, or simply being present, family support can ease the burden of adversity and enhance resilience.

• **Providing a Sense of Stability and Security**: Strong family relationships offer emotional security, vital for resilience. Knowing you have a stable support system to fall back on can give you the confidence to face challenges with courage and determination.

Healthy Family Communication

Open and healthy family communication is essential for building strong, supportive relationships to withstand life's challenges.

• **Active Listening and Expressing Empathy**: Encourage family members to listen actively to each other's concerns and express empathy. Creating an environment where everyone feels heard and understood strengthens family bonds and promotes emotional resilience.

• **Regular Family Meetings or Check-ins**: Scheduling regular family meetings allows members to discuss any issues or concerns openly. This practice fosters a sense of shared responsibility and ensures that problems are addressed before they escalate.

Strengthening Family Bonds

Investing in family relationships and cultivating a sense of togetherness is essential.

• **Shared Activities and Traditions**: Engage in regular family activities, such as dinners, vacations, or game nights, to build strong emotional connections. Family traditions, in particular, create a sense of continuity and shared identity that reinforces resilience.

• **Open and Honest Discussions About Feelings and Challenges**: Encourage family members to share their feelings and challenges openly. Honest conversations create a supportive environment where individuals can seek advice and comfort when needed.

Managing Family Conflict

Conflict is inevitable in any family, but learning how to resolve disputes constructively is crucial for maintaining strong family relationships.

• **Conflict Resolution Techniques**: Teach family members conflict resolution techniques, such as active listening, empathy, and compromise. Families can strengthen their bonds by resolving conflicts peacefully and creating a more resilient support system.

• **Seeking Family Therapy if Needed**: If conflicts persist and become detrimental to family relationships, consider seeking professional family therapy. A therapist can help family members work through issues and develop healthier communication patterns essential for long-term resilience.

Biblical Example: Jonathan and David – A Supportive Friendship

In **1 Samuel 18-20**, we find the story of **David** and **Jonathan**, which exemplifies the power of a solid and supportive friendship. David, the future king of Israel, and Jonathan, the son of King Saul, formed a deep and loyal bond despite their political tensions and potential rivalry.

Jonathan recognized David's anointing by God and supported him even though this meant his right to the throne would be passed over. In a time when David faced immense danger from King Saul's jealousy, Jonathan became David's advocate and protector, often risking his own life to help David escape from Saul's attempts to kill him.

In **1 Samuel 20**, Jonathan helps David confirm King Saul's intentions and ensures David's safety by devising a secret communication method using arrows. Their friendship was rooted in mutual respect, loyalty, and faith in God. Even in the face of immense personal and political challenges, Jonathan's unwavering support gave David the strength to endure one of the most challenging periods in his life.

This story illustrates how a supportive friendship can provide strength, guidance, and protection during hardship. David's journey to the throne was fraught with danger and uncertainty, but Jonathan's loyalty, counsel, and selflessness were essential in helping David navigate this period of his life. Their bond shows that a robust support system—especially one based on faith and loyalty—can be the difference between despair and triumph.

REFERENCES

Granovetter, M. S. (1973). The strength of weak ties. *American Journal of Sociology, 78*(6), 1360-1380.

4

EMOTIONAL REGULATION AND SELF-AWARENESS

One of the foundational aspects of resilience is the ability to regulate our emotions and cultivate a deep sense of self-awareness. Emotional regulation allows us to navigate challenges without being overwhelmed by negative feelings. Self-awareness helps us understand the roots of our emotions and take action to address them constructively. This chapter explores techniques to enhance emotional clarity, manage difficult emotions, and foster a positive internal dialogue. By developing these skills, we can build a more resilient mindset and effectively handle life's inevitable stressors.

Journaling for Emotional Clarity

Journaling is one of the most powerful tools for emotional clarity and self-reflection. It serves as a mirror for the mind, offering a safe space to express emotions, explore thoughts, and identify patterns in behavior. Regular journaling promotes emotional awareness, helping individuals to understand their feelings better and develop constructive ways of managing them.

- **Enhances Self-Understanding:** Writing down your thoughts and feelings can lead to profound insights into your emotional state. When you see your thoughts on paper, it becomes easier to recognize recurring themes, unresolved issues, or unacknowledged emotions. This increased self-awareness helps you understand the 'why' behind your reactions and empowers you to respond rather than react to situations.

• **Provides a Safe Outlet for Emotions:** Emotions can often feel overwhelming, especially in moments of stress. Journaling offers a private and non-judgmental outlet for expressing anger, sadness, or frustration. By putting your feelings into words, you create distance from them, allowing you to process them more effectively.

• **Helps Identify Patterns in Thoughts and Feelings:** Journaling can reveal patterns in your emotional responses over time. You might notice that specific triggers repeatedly lead to similar emotional outcomes, such as frustration or anxiety. Recognizing these patterns is the first step toward developing strategies to break them and foster more adaptive emotional responses.

Types of Journaling

Various approaches to journaling can aid emotional clarity. Depending on your preferences, you can experiment with different types of journaling until you find the best method for you.

• **Free Writing:** In this method, you write continuously without concern for grammar, structure, or logic. The goal is to let your thoughts flow freely onto the page. Free writing can help uncover unconscious thoughts and emotions, making it a valuable tool for self-discovery.

• **Prompt-Based Journaling:** This method involves responding to specific prompts to guide reflection. Prompts might focus on your emotions, relationships, or current challenges. Prompt-based journaling can provide structure for those who find it difficult to start writing.

• **Gratitude Journaling:** This practice involves writing down things you are grateful for daily. Gratitude journaling enhances mood, reduces stress, and fosters a positive outlook. By focusing on the positive aspects of your life, you can shift your perspective away from stressors and challenges.

Journaling Prompts

To get started with journaling, consider using the following prompts:

- "What am I feeling right now and why?"
- "What are three things I am grateful for today?"
- "Describe a recent challenge and how I handled it."

These prompts encourage reflection on one's current emotional state, help one cultivate gratitude, and assess how one has navigated recent challenges.

Incorporating Journaling into Your Daily Routine

It is essential to incorporate journaling into your daily routine. Here are a few strategies to help make journaling a regular practice:

- **Set Aside a Specific Time Each Day:** Designate a specific time, whether it's in the morning or before bed, to sit down and write. Creating consistency helps establish journaling as a habit.

- **Create a Comfortable Journaling Space:** Choose a quiet and comfortable place to focus on your writing without distractions. This could be a cozy corner of your home or a favorite spot in nature.

- **Use Digital Tools or Apps for Journaling:** If pen and paper aren't your preferred method, consider using digital journaling apps like Day One or Penzu. These tools offer prompts, reminders, and the ability to organize your thoughts digitally.

Cognitive Restructuring Techniques

Cognitive restructuring is a technique for challenging and changing negative thought patterns. This process plays a crucial role in emotional regulation by helping individuals recognize and reframe distorted thoughts that lead to negative emotions. Cognitive restructuring improves emotional well-being and problem-solving abilities by replacing unhelpful thoughts with more balanced and realistic ones.

- **Changing Negative Thought Patterns:** At the core of cognitive restructuring is identifying and changing negative or irrational thoughts. These thoughts often arise automatically in response to stress or difficult situations and can significantly influence how we feel and act. By learning to question these thoughts, we can reduce their impact and prevent them from spiraling into emotional distress.

• **Enhancing Problem-Solving Abilities**: Cognitive restructuring also promotes more effective problem-solving. With a calmer and more balanced mindset, we are likelier to find solutions to challenges. Reframing our thoughts can reduce a situation's emotional charge and focus on practical steps forward.

Identifying Distorted Thoughts

The first step in cognitive restructuring is recognizing cognitive distortions, such as irrational and biased thinking. Common cognitive distortions include:

• **All-or-Nothing Thinking**: You view situations in black-and-white terms, with no middle ground. For example, thinking, "If I don't succeed perfectly, I'm a failure."

• **Overgeneralization**: Drawing broad, negative conclusions based on a single event, such as "I made a mistake today, so I'll never be good at this."

• **Catastrophizing**: Expecting the worst possible outcome in a situation, such as assuming that making a small error at work will lead to losing your job.

Challenging Negative Thoughts

Once you've identified a distorted thought, the next step is to challenge it by questioning the accuracy of the thought and considering alternative, more balanced perspectives. To do this, you can ask yourself:

• **What evidence do I have that this thought is true?**

• **What evidence do I have that this thought is false?**

• **Is there another way to view this situation?**

By examining the evidence for and against your thought, you can often see that the negative thought is exaggerated or inaccurate.

Practical Exercises

Here are a few exercises that can help you practice cognitive restructuring:

• **Thought Record Worksheets:** These guide you through identifying and challenging negative thoughts. You can practice reframing distorted thinking by writing down your thoughts, the evidence for and against them, and alternative perspectives.

• **Role-Playing Scenarios:** Practicing cognitive restructuring through role-playing can help you rehearse challenging situations in a controlled environment. By working through hypothetical scenarios, you can develop more adaptive responses to stress.

• **The ABCDE Model:** This cognitive restructuring tool breaks down the process of reframing thoughts into five steps: Activating event, Belief, Consequence, Disputation, and Effect. Following this model, you can systematically work through negative thoughts and reach more balanced conclusions.

Mindfulness Meditation for Emotional Balance

Mindfulness meditation is another powerful tool for emotional regulation. By focusing on the present moment and observing thoughts and emotions without judgment, Mindfulness helps reduce emotional reactivity and promotes inner calm. It teaches individuals to step back from their feelings and observe them as passing experiences rather than becoming overwhelmed.

• **Focuses on Present Moment Awareness:** Mindfulness meditation emphasizes being fully present in the here and now, which helps break the cycle of rumination about the past or anxiety about the future. By anchoring attention to the present, Mindfulness creates space for more measured and thoughtful responses to stress.

• **Reduces Emotional Reactivity:** One of Mindfulness's most profound benefits is its ability to reduce emotional reactivity. Through regular practice, Mindfulness increases emotional awareness and enhances the ability to pause before reacting to challenging situations, allowing for more intentional and constructive responses.

Mindfulness Practices

Here are a few Mindfulness meditation techniques that can help regulate emotions:

• **Breath Awareness Meditation:** This practice involves focusing on your breath and observing each inhalation and exhalation without trying to change it. Focusing on the breath, you center your attention and calm the mind.

• **Body Scan Meditation:** In this technique, you mentally scan your body from head to toe, noticing any tension or discomfort. This practice promotes relaxation and increases awareness of how stress affects the body.

• **Loving-Kindness Meditation:** This meditation focuses on cultivating compassion for yourself and others by silently repeating phrases like, "May I be happy, may I be healthy, may I be at peace," and extending these wishes to others. Loving-kindness meditation fosters empathy and emotional connection.

Daily Integration

Mindfulness meditation becomes part of your daily life through tiny, consistent practices:

• **Short Meditation Sessions:** Start with brief sessions of 5-10 minutes each day. Even a few minutes of mindful breathing or meditation can significantly benefit emotional regulation.

• **Mindful Breathing During Breaks:** Take moments to practice mindful breathing during breaks throughout the day. Whether at work or home, this can help reset your mind and emotions, especially during stressful moments.

Scientific Support for Mindfulness

Numerous studies have demonstrated the effectiveness of Mindfulness in reducing stress, anxiety, and depression. Research has shown that regular Mindfulness practice leads to changes in brain structure, particularly in areas related to emotional regulation (Hölzel et al., 2011). A meta-analysis of Mindfulness-based therapies also found that these practices significantly reduced symptoms of anxiety and depression while also improving emotional resilience and overall mental health (Hofmann et al., 2010). These studies underscore the value of Mindfulness as a practical tool for emotional regulation, particularly in the face of life's challenges.

Recognizing and Managing Triggers

Emotional triggers are events, people, or situations that elicit strong emotional responses, often due to unresolved issues or past experiences. Recognizing and managing these triggers is essential for emotional regulation, as unchecked triggers can lead to overwhelming reactions and prevent individuals from responding thoughtfully.

- **Identifying Emotional Triggers:** The first step in managing emotional triggers is recognizing them. Emotional triggers can manifest in both physical and emotional signs, such as increased heart rate, muscle tension, or feelings of anxiety and anger. Familiar sources of triggers include certain people (e.g., a difficult colleague), specific situations (e.g., public speaking), or memories of past events. By identifying the patterns that activate these solid emotional responses, you gain the awareness necessary to intervene before your emotions escalate.

- **Physical and Emotional Signs of Being Triggered:** Triggers often manifest physically before we fully recognize them emotionally. Common physical signs include a racing heart, shallow breathing, or muscle tension. Emotional signs might consist of feelings of anxiety, fear, frustration, or anger. These early warning signs are critical to managing emotional responses before they become overwhelming.

Managing Triggers

Once you've identified your triggers, the next step is to manage them effectively. Emotional regulation techniques can help you stay grounded and respond to triggers more measuredly rather than impulsively.

- **Deep Breathing and Grounding Techniques:** Deep breathing exercises help activate the parasympathetic nervous system, which calms the body and mind. When you feel triggered, taking a few deep, slow breaths can quickly reduce the intensity of your emotional response. Grounding techniques, such as focusing on your surroundings or sensations, can bring you back to the present moment and diffuse the emotional charge.

• **Cognitive Reframing**: Cognitive reframing involves challenging the thoughts that arise when you are triggered. For example, if a specific situation makes you anxious, you can ask yourself, "Is this reaction proportional to the situation?" By reframing your thoughts and viewing the problem from a different perspective, you can reduce the emotional impact of the trigger.

• **Taking a Break or Removing Yourself from the Situation**: Sometimes, the best way to manage a trigger is to step away from the situation. Taking a break allows you to regroup and process your emotions in a calmer environment, preventing impulsive reactions that might escalate the situation.

Developing an Action Plan

Creating a personalized action plan for dealing with triggers can help you manage emotional responses more effectively. This plan should include steps for identifying triggers, responding constructively, and practicing coping strategies in advance.

• **Identifying Specific Triggers**: List the people, situations, or events that commonly trigger you. The more specific you can be, the better equipped you'll be to manage these triggers when they arise.

• **Planning Responses to Triggers**: Develop a response plan for each trigger. These might involve using deep breathing techniques, removing yourself from the situation, or engaging in positive self-talk to calm your emotions.

• **Practicing Coping Strategies in Advance**: To ensure your action plan is effective, practice your coping strategies regularly. The more you rehearse these techniques, the easier it will be to use them in emotional distress.

Real-Life Examples

Here are two examples of individuals successfully managing their emotional triggers:

- **A Professional Managing Stress Triggers at Work:** Marketing executive Saarya often felt overwhelmed during high-pressure meetings. She noticed that her trigger was the fear of being judged by her peers. Saarya learned to calm her nerves before meetings using deep breathing and cognitive reframing. She reminded herself that mistakes were part of the learning process and focused on contributing her insights without worrying about judgment.
- **Someone Coping with Social Anxiety in Public Settings:** David struggled with social anxiety, especially in crowded events. He recognized that large gatherings triggered feelings of insecurity and fear of rejection. David began using grounding techniques, such as focusing on his breath and engaging in small talk to ease his nerves. By practicing these strategies, he could stay present and enjoy social interactions without anxiety.

The Role of Self-Compassion in Resilience

Self-compassion is treating oneself with kindness, understanding, and acceptance, especially in times of failure or difficulty. It involves recognizing that suffering and imperfection are part of the human experience rather than something to be judged or criticized. Self-compassion is crucial to resilience because it helps individuals recover from setbacks without self-blame or harsh judgment.

- **Treating Oneself with Kindness and Understanding:** Self-compassion means offering yourself the kindness and care you would offer a friend. When faced with adversity or failure, practice being gentle and understanding instead of criticizing yourself. Create a supportive internal environment where emotional healing can take place.
- **Recognizing Common Humanity:** A central component of self-compassion is recognizing that everyone experiences hardship and failure. You are not alone in your struggles. This perspective fosters a sense of connectedness and reduces feelings of isolation, which can exacerbate stress and emotional pain.
- **Practicing Mindfulness:** Mindfulness plays a crucial role in

self-compassion by encouraging individuals to acknowledge their emotions without becoming overwhelmed. Mindfulness teaches us to observe our feelings with curiosity and acceptance rather than judgment, allowing us to process difficult emotions without being consumed by them.

Benefits of Self-Compassion

Research has shown that self-compassion has many psychological benefits, especially for emotional resilience.

• **Reduced Self-Criticism**: Self-compassion minimizes the tendency to engage in harsh self-criticism, which can erode self-esteem and emotional well-being. By treating yourself with kindness, you cultivate a sense of inner strength and acceptance.

• **Increased Emotional Resilience**: Self-compassion fosters emotional resilience by helping individuals recover from failure or adversity more quickly. When you approach challenges with self-compassion, you are less likely to be paralyzed by fear of failure and more likely to learn from your experiences.

• **Enhanced Overall Well-Being**: Numerous studies have shown that individuals who practice self-compassion experience greater overall well-being, including lower anxiety levels, depression, and stress (Neff, 2011). Self-compassion produces higher levels of happiness, life satisfaction, and emotional balance.

Practicing Self-Compassion

Here are some practical ways to cultivate self-compassion:

• **Self-Compassionate Letter Writing**: One way to practice self-compassion is to write a letter to yourself as though you were comforting a friend. In this letter, express understanding, kindness, and support for your difficulties.

• **Loving-Kindness Meditation Focused on Oneself**: This meditation focuses on directing feelings of kindness and love toward yourself. Repeat phrases like, "May I be happy, may I be healthy, may I be at peace." This practice fosters self-acceptance and reduces feelings of self-judgment.

• **Self-Compassion Breaks During Stressful Times**: When you encounter a stressful situation, take a moment to pause and remind yourself that it's okay to feel overwhelmed. Offer yourself words of encouragement and understanding, such as, "This is a hard moment, but I can get through it with kindness and patience."

Scientific Evidence

Research supports the role of self-compassion in promoting emotional resilience. Studies have shown that individuals who practice self-compassion experience lower levels of anxiety, depression, and stress while also exhibiting more robust emotional stability (Neff & Germer, 2013). Self-compassion produces better coping mechanisms and an increased ability to recover from adversity (Gilbert & Procter, 2006).

Developing a Positive Internal Dialogue

Our internal dialogue—how we talk to ourselves—profoundly impacts our emotional well-being and resilience. Positive internal dialogue can boost self-esteem, foster emotional balance, and help us navigate difficult situations confidently. Conversely, negative self-talk can lead to feelings of inadequacy, anxiety, and depression.

- **Influences Self-Esteem and Self-Worth:** How we speak to ourselves directly affects our feelings. Positive internal dialogue builds self-esteem and a sense of self-worth, while negative self-talk can undermine confidence and contribute to self-doubt.

- **Impacts Emotional Responses and Behavior:** Our thoughts shape our emotions, and our feelings influence our behavior. We can foster more adaptive emotional responses and make healthier decisions by cultivating a positive internal dialogue.

Recognizing Negative Self-Talk

Negative self-talk often arises unconsciously but significantly impacts how we feel and behave. Common types of negative self-talk include:

- **"I Can't Do This":** A self-defeating thought that undermines confidence and prevents you from taking action.

- **"I'm Not Good Enough":** A pervasive feeling of inadequacy that can lead to hopelessness or despair.

Recognizing these patterns is the first step in transforming them into more constructive and empowering thoughts.

Reframing Negative Thoughts

Once you've identified negative self-talk, the next step is to reframe it. Replace negative thoughts with positive affirmations that reflect your strengths and potential.

- **Examples of Positive Affirmations:**
  ○ "I am capable of handling this challenge."
  ○ "I am worthy of love and respect."
  ○ "I have the strength to overcome this difficulty."

Creating a Positive Mindset

Here are some strategies for maintaining a positive internal dialogue:

- **Keeping a Positivity Journal:** Much like gratitude journaling, a positivity journal involves daily writing down positive thoughts and experiences. This practice reinforces a positive mindset and helps shift your focus away from negative self-talk. Reflecting on small wins, personal strengths, and moments of joy can build your resilience and make it easier to maintain an optimistic outlook during challenging times.

- **Surrounding Yourself with Positive Influences:** The people you surround yourself with can significantly impact your internal dialogue. Spending time with individuals who uplift and encourage you fosters positive thinking and reinforces your self-worth. Conversely, negative influences may contribute to self-doubt and pessimism. Be mindful of your social circles and seek relationships supporting your emotional well-being.

- **Engaging in Activities that Boost Self-Esteem:** Participating in activities that make you feel capable and empowered is essential for developing a positive mindset. Whether pursuing a hobby you love, volunteering, or learning new skills, fulfilling activities help reinforce your strengths and build confidence.

Embracing Emotional Regulation and Self-Awareness

The ability to regulate emotions and cultivate self-awareness is foundational to building resilience. As explored in this chapter, emotional regulation involves recognizing and managing difficult emotions, while self-awareness allows us to understand the patterns behind our reactions. By practicing techniques such as journaling, cognitive restructuring, Mindfulness meditation, and self-compassion, we can develop a more profound sense of emotional balance and foster a positive internal dialogue.

Emotional regulation and self-awareness are not innate traits but skills that can be learned and refined over time. Through consistent practice, we can become more adept at managing stress, navigating challenges, and recovering from setbacks with grace and composure. Incorporating these practices into your daily life builds the emotional strength and resilience to face life's inevitable ups and downs successfully.

Remember that resilience is not about avoiding difficulty but about growing through it. With the tools outlined in this chapter, you are well on your way to becoming more self-aware and emotionally balanced, empowering yourself to live a more resilient and fulfilled life.

Biblical Example: David's Emotional Regulation in the Psalms

The Bible offers a powerful example of emotional regulation and self-awareness through the life of David, particularly in the Psalms. David, who faced numerous challenges, including persecution, betrayal, and personal failures, expressed his emotions honestly and openly in his writings. The Psalms serve as a form of journaling, where David poured out his heart to God, reflecting on his fears, anxieties, and moments of despair and finding comfort, strength, and hope.

One poignant example can be found in **Psalm 42**, where David writes:

"Why, my soul, are you downcast? Why so disturbed
within me? Put your hope in God, for I will yet
praise him, my Savior and my God." *(Psalm
42:11, NIV)*

In this verse, David acknowledges his emotional state with complete honesty, asking himself why he feels so distressed. Yet, he doesn't stop there. He challenges his negative thoughts by reminding himself to place his hope in God, choosing to focus on God's faithfulness rather than the weight of his present emotions. This shift is a clear example of cognitive restructuring, as David shifts his perspective from despair to trust in God's promises.

David's journey through the Psalms reflects both the emotional clarity of journaling and the power of Mindfulness—present-moment awareness of his feelings—and reframing his thoughts through faith. His deep self-awareness and trust in God allowed him to regulate his emotions in the face of overwhelming adversity. David's Psalms remind us that emotional regulation is not about suppressing emotions but about engaging with them honestly and finding strength through faith and reflection.

REFERENCES

Gilbert, P., & Procter, S. (2006). Compassionate mind training for people with high shame and self-criticism: Overview and pilot study of a group therapy approach. *Clinical Psychology & Psychotherapy, 13*(6), 353-379.

Hofmann, S. G., Sawyer, A. T., Witt, A. A., & Oh, D. (2010). The effect of Mindfulness-based therapy on anxiety and depression: A meta-analytic review. *Journal of Consulting and Clinical Psychology, 78*(2), 169-183.

Hölzel, B. K., Carmody, J., Evans, K. C., Hoge, E. A., Dusek, J. A., Morgan, L., ... & Lazar, S. W. (2011). Stress reduction correlates with structural changes in the amygdala. *Social Cognitive and Affective Neuroscience, 5*(1), 11-17.

Neff, K. D. (2011). Self-compassion, self-esteem, and well-being. *Social and Personality Psychology Compass, 5*(1), 1-12.

Neff, K. D., & Germer, C. K. (2013). A pilot study and randomized controlled trial of the mindful self-compassion program. *Journal of Clinical Psychology, 69*(1), 28-44.

PLEASE SHARE

If you have found value in this book, please share your experience by leaving a rating or review on Amazon.

If you are reading an ebook, please click this link go to your review page.

If you are reading a print book, point your phone's camera at the QR code below to be taken to your review page. Thank you!

5

OVERCOMING FEAR OF FAILURE AND PROCRASTINATION

This chapter will explore how fear of failure and procrastination often work together, creating mental hurdles that block progress. By understanding the psychological mechanisms behind these behaviors and implementing practical strategies like cognitive reframing, goal-setting, and incremental improvement, you can learn to overcome these challenges. Combining these strategies with a faith-based approach will help you develop resilience in your personal and professional life.

Reframing Negative Thoughts

Fear of failure often finds its roots in negative thought patterns that distort reality and amplify perceived risks. These thoughts can lead to procrastination as a defense mechanism to avoid potential failure. However, by understanding these cognitive distortions and learning how to reframe them, you can change how you perceive challenges and reduce the emotional burden of failure. This understanding and reframing can bring a sense of relief, empowering you to take control of your thoughts and actions.

- **Understanding Negative Thought Patterns:** Negative thought patterns are cognitive distortions that exacerbate fear and anxiety. These can take various forms, such as all-or-nothing thinking (believing that if you don't succeed perfectly, you've failed), catastrophizing (thinking that if something goes wrong, it will be a disaster), and overgeneralization (assuming that because you failed once, you'll always fail). Recognizing these common distortions is the first step in overcoming the fear of failure (Beck, 1976; Burns, 1989).

- **Impact on Behavior and Performance:** These distorted thoughts directly affect behavior, often leading to avoidance and procrastination. Research shows that individuals who experience high levels of fear of failure are more likely to procrastinate to protect themselves from the possibility of failing (Steel, 2007). Procrastination, in turn, leads to decreased performance, increased stress, and reinforcement of negative self-beliefs.

TECHNIQUES FOR REFRAMING Negative Thoughts

Reframing negative thoughts is a crucial cognitive-behavioral strategy for overcoming the fear of failure. Cognitive restructuring, a key component of this strategy, involves challenging the validity of negative thoughts and replacing them with more balanced, realistic alternatives. This process helps to break the cycle of negative thinking and reduce the emotional burden of failure.

- **Cognitive Restructuring Exercises:** One practical reframing approach is to ask yourself, "What evidence supports this thought?" and "What evidence contradicts it?" For example, if you think, "I'll never succeed in this task," consider past experiences where you overcame challenges, providing evidence that counters the negative belief (Beck, 1976).

- **Positive Affirmations:** Another tool for reframing is using positive affirmations. Repeating statements like "I am capable of learning and growing" or "Setbacks are a part of the process" can help reinforce a growth mindset, which is essential for resilience (Dweck, 2006).

. . .

Practical Examples

- **A Student Using Positive Affirmations Before Exams:** Maria, a university student, struggled with exam anxiety due to the fear of failing. Her automatic thought was, "If I don't do well, it will ruin my future." By practicing positive affirmations such as, "I have studied and am prepared, and I will do my best," she managed her anxiety and improved her performance (Seligman, 2011).

- **An Employee Reframing Thoughts About a Challenging Project:** John, a marketing executive, was assigned a high-stakes project at work. His initial thought was, "If I mess this up, I'll lose my job." By applying cognitive restructuring, he reframed his thinking to, "This project is a learning opportunity, and I can manage challenges with support from my team." This reframing helped him approach the project with a more positive mindset (Bandura, 1997).

Scientific Evidence

Scientific research supports the effectiveness of cognitive restructuring techniques. A meta-analysis of cognitive-behavioral therapy (CBT) found that restructuring negative thoughts reduces anxiety and improves performance across various domains (Butler et al., 2006). Moreover, studies show positive self-talk and affirmations enhance self-efficacy, leading to greater confidence and resilience in stressful situations (Sherman et al., 2009).

Setting SMART Goals

One of the most practical ways to combat procrastination and fear of failure is by setting SMART goals. SMART goals—Specific, Measurable, Achievable, Relevant, and Time-bound—provide clarity and structure, helping individuals break down large tasks into manageable steps.

- **Introduction to SMART Goals:** Setting clear, realistic goals is essential for overcoming the fear of failure. Research indicates that individuals who set specific and achievable goals are more likely to succeed, as such goals reduce uncertainty and increase focus (Locke & Latham, 2002).

Creating **SMART Goals**

A step-by-step guide to setting SMART goals includes:

1 **Specific:** Define what you want to achieve. Vague goals such as "get healthier" lack direction. Instead, opt for a particular goal like "exercise thrice weekly."

2 **Measurable:** Determine how you will measure progress. For instance, track your workout sessions or progress on a work project.

3 **Achievable:** Set realistic goals. While it is essential to challenge yourself, setting unattainable goals can trigger fear of failure and further procrastination (Bandura, 1997).

4 **Relevant:** Ensure the goal aligns with your long-term aspirations. For example, if you aim to advance in your career, set goals related to skill development or networking.

5 **Time-bound:** Set a deadline to create a sense of urgency and maintain momentum.

Examples of **SMART Goals**

Here are a few examples of SMART goals in different areas of life:

• **Career Goal:** "Complete a certification course within six months to enhance my qualifications for a promotion."

• **Personal Goal:** "Exercise for 30 minutes thrice a week for three months to improve my fitness."

Benefits of **SMART Goals**

Setting SMART goals increases clarity and reduces the fear of failure by providing clear markers of success. SMART goals help break down overwhelming tasks, making them more achievable and enhancing motivation (Locke & Latham, 2006). Individuals can stay engaged and committed while reducing procrastination by focusing on incremental progress.

The Power of Incremental Progress

Fear of failure often stems from viewing goals as too large or unattainable. However, breaking down goals into smaller, manageable steps, known as incremental progress, helps reduce overwhelm and builds momentum. This reassurance and encouragement can help you stay focused and committed to your goals.

Incremental progress, a key concept in overcoming fear of failure and procrastination, refers to taking small, consistent actions toward larger goals. Each small success, no matter how minor, builds confidence and makes the overall goal more achievable. By focusing on these small wins, you can reduce overwhelm and build momentum towards your larger goals (Amabile & Kramer, 2011).

Breaking Down Goals

When breaking down larger goals, consider the following strategies:

• **Create a Task List:** Write down all the small steps necessary to achieve your goal. The list provides a roadmap and makes the process less intimidating.

• **Set Daily or Weekly Milestones:** Rather than focusing on the end result, set smaller milestones to achieve regularly. For instance, if you want to write a book, set a daily word count goal, such as 500 words.

Tracking Progress

Tracking progress helps maintain motivation by providing

tangible evidence of achievement. Here are a few methods to track progress:

- **Using Journals or Apps:** Many individuals successfully track their progress using apps such as Trello or Todoist or by keeping a progress journal (Amabile & Kramer, 2011).

- **Celebrating Small Wins:** Reward yourself for reaching smaller milestones. These rewards can range from small treats to simply taking a break, and they help reinforce positive behavior (Seligman, 2011).

REAL-LIFE EXAMPLES

- **A Writer Completing a Book by Writing a Set Number of Words Daily:** Jessica, an aspiring author, was overwhelmed by the idea of writing a full-length novel. Instead of focusing on the final goal, she broke it down into smaller steps by committing to writing 500 words a day. This approach reduced her fear of failure and made the writing process more manageable (Amabile & Kramer, 2011).

- **A Fitness Enthusiast Reaching Their Goal Through Gradual Increases:** Tom wanted to improve his fitness level but felt discouraged by his initial inability to complete long runs. By setting incremental goals, such as running one mile a day and gradually increasing the distance, he eventually achieved his goal of running a marathon (Dweck, 2006).

Overcoming Procrastination: Practical Steps

Procrastination often stems from a fear of failure or feeling over-whelmed by large tasks. By understanding the psychology behind procrastination, you can implement practical techniques to overcome it.

- **Understanding Procrastination:** Procrastination is often a way to avoid anxiety associated with tasks perceived as complicated or high-stakes. However, it can also lead to increased stress, reduced productivity, and a greater likelihood of failure (Steel, 2007).

. . .

PRACTICAL TECHNIQUES TO **Overcome Procrastination**

Here are some actionable strategies for overcoming procrastination:

• **The "Two-Minute Rule":** Do it immediately if a task takes less than two minutes. This rule helps prevent small tasks from piling up and becoming overwhelming (Allen, 2001).

• **Time Management Techniques:** Methods like the **Pomodoro Technique** (working for 25-minute intervals followed by a short break) can help break tasks into manageable segments, making them less daunting (Cirillo, 2006).

• **Setting Specific Deadlines:** Research shows that self-imposed deadlines can significantly reduce procrastination by creating a sense of urgency and accountability (Ariely & Wertenbroch, 2002).

TOOLS AND RESOURCES

Here are a few tools and resources to help manage procrastination:

• **Productivity Apps:** Apps like **Todoist, Trello,** or **Focus@Will** provide task management systems that can break larger projects into smaller, manageable tasks and help you track progress over time. These apps allow you to set deadlines and reminders, ensuring tasks do not slip through the cracks (Cirillo, 2006).

• **Accountability Partners or Groups:** Having someone hold you accountable can significantly reduce procrastination. Research shows that individuals who share their goals with others and receive regular check-ins are more likely to complete their tasks on time (Locke & Latham, 2002).

REAL-LIFE STRATEGIES

Real-world applications of these techniques highlight their effectiveness:

• **A Student Using the Pomodoro Technique for Studying**: Tim, a college student, struggled with procrastination during exam preparation. Using the Pomodoro Technique, he broke down his study sessions into 25-minute intervals, with short breaks. This structured approach helped him stay focused and manage his time effectively, improving his exam performance (Cirillo, 2006).

• **A Professional Using Accountability Partners for Project Deadlines**: Jane, a project manager, often procrastinated on essential tasks. To combat this, she joined an accountability group with colleagues who held weekly check-ins to review progress. This external motivation helped her stay on track and complete her projects on time (Locke & Latham, 2002).

The Science of Motivation: What Drives Us

Motivation plays a crucial role in overcoming the fear of failure and procrastination. Understanding the different types of motivation and their theories can help you harness your internal drive to achieve your goals.

• **Intrinsic vs. Extrinsic Motivation**: Intrinsic motivation arises from internal satisfaction or enjoyment of a task, while extrinsic motivation is driven by external rewards or pressures (Deci & Ryan, 1985). Research suggests that intrinsic motivation is more sustainable and leads to better long-term success, as individuals are more likely to persist when they find personal value in their tasks (Ryan & Deci, 2000).

MOTIVATION THEORIES

Here are two fundamental theories of motivation that can help to overcome the fear of failure:

• **Self-Determination Theory**: This theory emphasizes the importance of autonomy, competence, and relatedness in fostering intrinsic motivation. When individuals feel they have control over their goals (autonomy), believe they are capable (competence), and feel connected to others (relatedness), they are more likely to stay motivated (Deci & Ryan, 1985).

• **Maslow's Hierarchy of Needs**: According to Maslow, individuals are motivated to fulfill basic needs (such as safety and security) before focusing on higher-order goals like self-actualization (Maslow, 1943). Understanding where you are in this hierarchy can help you identify what might be blocking your motivation.

PRACTICAL STRATEGIES **for Harnessing Motivation**

Here are some actionable strategies for increasing motivation:

• **Setting Meaningful and Challenging Goals**: Goals that are personally meaningful and provide a sense of challenge are more likely to inspire motivation. Research shows that individuals are more engaged and motivated when their tasks align with their values (Locke & Latham, 2002).

• **Finding Intrinsic Rewards in Tasks**: An intrinsic reward can boost motivation even in mundane or tedious tasks. For example, if you are working on a long project, focus on the satisfaction of learning or growing through the process rather than just the external reward.

• **Creating a Supportive Environment**: Surround yourself with supportive individuals and create an environment that fosters focus and discipline. Whether it is a quiet workspace or a network of encouraging peers, your environment can significantly influence your motivation levels (Ryan & Deci, 2000).

SCIENTIFIC STUDIES

Studies show that individuals who set clear goals and work towards intrinsic rewards are more likely to stay motivated and achieve long-term success (Deci & Ryan, 1985). Additionally, research on motivation and procrastination demonstrates that those with higher intrinsic motivation are less likely to delay tasks as they derive personal satisfaction from completing them (Steel, 2007).

Learning from Setbacks: Turning Failure into Success

Reframing failure as a learning opportunity is a key to overcoming the fear of failure and developing resilience. The concept of "failing forward" emphasizes that each setback is a step towards growth and eventual success.

- **Reframing Failure:** Instead of viewing failure as a personal deficiency, approach it as a chance to learn and improve. This mindset shift is central to the **growth mindset**—the belief that abilities can be developed through dedication and hard work (Dweck, 2006).

ANALYZING SETBACKS

When you encounter failure, use the following steps to analyze and learn from the experience:

1 **Identify What Went Wrong:** Objectively assess the situation to understand why the outcome did not meet your expectations. Was it due to external factors, or could you improve your approach?

2 **Reflect on What Could Be Done Differently:** Consider how to handle similar situations. Would more preparation help? Could you break the task into smaller steps next time?

DEVELOPING Resilience

Learning from setbacks builds resilience by reinforcing perseverance and flexibility. Research on resilience highlights the importance of adapting to challenges and viewing failures as opportunities for growth (Masten, 2001). The ability to stay focused despite setbacks increases the likelihood of long-term success.

INSPIRATIONAL STORIES

History is filled with stories of individuals who turned failure into success:

- **Thomas Edison's Multiple Attempts Before Inventing the Light Bulb**: Edison famously said, "I have not failed. I've just found 10,000 ways that won't work." Despite numerous failures, his persistence eventually led to the invention of the light bulb (Macleod, 2005).
- **J.K. Rowling's Rejections Before Publishing Harry Potter**: Rowling's manuscript for *Harry Potter* was rejected by multiple publishers. Instead of giving up, she persisted, and the series eventually became a global phenomenon (Smith, 2017).

Biblical Example: Peter's Redemption After Failure

In the Bible, the Apostle Peter is a powerful example of overcoming the fear of failure. Peter, one of Jesus' closest disciples, famously denied Jesus three times during a moment of fear and weakness (Luke 22:54-62). His failure was profound, but it did not define him. After Jesus' resurrection, Peter was allowed to redeem himself. Jesus asked Peter three times, "Do you love me?" and each time, Peter affirmed his love and commitment (John 21:15-17). This moment was a turning point for Peter, and he became a crucial leader in the early Christian church.

Peter's story demonstrates that failure is not the end of the journey. Like Peter, we can learn from our mistakes, grow in our faith, and continue to pursue our purpose with renewed determination. Peter's ability to overcome his fear of failure and seek redemption teaches us that resilience and perseverance are essential to fulfilling our potential.

REFERENCES

Amabile, T. M., & Kramer, S. J. (2011). *The Progress Principle: Using Small Wins to Ignite Joy, Engagement, and Creativity at Work*. Harvard Business Review Press.

Ariely, D., & Wertenbroch, K. (2002). Procrastination, deadlines, and performance: Self-control by precommitment. *Psychological Science, 13*(3), 219-224.

Bandura, A. (1997). *Self-Efficacy: The Exercise of Control*. Freeman.

Beck, A. T. (1976). *Cognitive Therapy and the Emotional Disorders*. International Universities Press.

Butler, A. C., Chapman, J. E., Forman, E. M., & Beck, A. T. (2006). The empirical status of cognitive-behavioral therapy: A review of meta-analyses. *Clinical Psychology Review, 26*(1), 17–31.

Burns, D. D. (1989). *The Feeling Good Handbook*. William Morrow.

Cirillo, F. (2006). *The Pomodoro Technique*. FC Garage.

Deci, E. L., & Ryan, R. M. (1985). *Intrinsic Motivation and Self-Determination in Human Behavior*. Springer Science & Business Media.

Dweck, C. S. (2006). *Mindset: The New Psychology of Success*. Random House.

Locke, E. A., & Latham, G. P. (2002). Building a practically useful theory of goal setting and task motivation: A 35-year odyssey. *American Psychologist, 57*(9), 705–717.

Locke, E. A., & Latham, G. P. (2006). New directions in goal-setting theory. *Current Directions in Psychological Science, 15*(5), 265–268.

Macleod, D. (2005). Edison's Light Bulb. *Smithsonian Institution*.

Masten, A. S. (2001). Ordinary magic: Resilience processes in development. *American Psychologist, 56*(3), 227-238.

Maslow, A. H. (1943). A theory of human motivation. *Psychological Review, 50*(4), 370–396.

Ryan, R. M., & Deci, E. L. (2000). Self-determination theory and the facilitation of intrinsic motivation, social development, and well-being. *American Psychologist, 55*(1), 68–78.

Seligman, M. E. P. (2011). *Flourish: A Visionary New Understanding of Happiness and Well-being*. Free Press.

Sherman, D. K., Cohen, G. L., Nelson, L. D., Nussbaum, A. D., Bunyan, D. P., & Garcia, J. (2009). Affirmed yet unaware: Exploring the role of awareness in the process of self-affirmation. *Journal of Personality and Social Psychology, 97*(5), 745-764.

Smith, A. (2017). *J.K. Rowling: A Biography*. Greenwood Biographies.

Steel, P. (2007). The nature of procrastination: A meta-analytic and theoretical review of quintessential self-regulatory failure. *Psychological Bulletin, 133*(1), 65-94.

6

ADAPTABILITY AND FLEXIBILITY IN CHANGING TIMES

In today's rapidly evolving world, adaptability and flexibility are critical components of resilience. These traits enable individuals to respond effectively to changes in personal life, professional settings, or the broader societal landscape. This chapter explores how embracing change, developing problem-solving skills, and fostering flexibility can help build resilience in uncertainty.

Embracing Change: A Mindset Shift

Change is an inevitable part of life, yet it often meets resistance due to the fear and anxiety it can provoke. Developing a positive attitude toward change is essential for resilience, as it allows us to perceive challenges as opportunities for growth rather than threats to stability.

- **Importance of Embracing Change:** Embracing change reduces the fear and anxiety associated with uncertainty, making it easier to navigate life's transitions. When we resist change, we create additional stress, impacting our mental and physical well-being (Smith et al., 2018). By viewing change as an opportunity, we open ourselves up to new possibilities and experiences that can enrich our lives.

- **Recognizing Opportunities Within Challenges:** Every change presents an opportunity, even if it initially seems complicated. These challenges can lead to personal and professional growth, whether learning a new skill, meeting new people, or adapting to a new environment. Research shows that individuals who embrace change are more likely to develop a growth mindset, which enhances their ability to learn and adapt (Dweck, 2006).

Growth Mindset vs. Fixed Mindset

Adopting a **growth mindset** is a powerful way to foster adaptability. Unlike a fixed mindset, which views abilities as static and unchangeable, a growth mindset believes skills and intelligence develop through effort and learning.

- **Characteristics of a Growth Mindset:** People with a growth mindset see challenges as opportunities to learn, embrace feedback, and persist in facing setbacks. They understand that failure is not a reflection of their intrinsic ability but a step toward improvement (Dweck, 2006). In contrast, individuals with a fixed mindset avoid challenges and often give up easily, fearing failure.

- **Benefits of Adopting a Growth Mindset:** A growth mindset allows individuals to be more adaptable, flexible, and open to learning new things. It leads to greater resilience, as setbacks are viewed as part of the growth process rather than insurmountable obstacles. Research supports the idea that those with a growth mindset are better equipped to handle change and uncertainty (Yeager & Dweck, 2012).

Techniques for Mindset Shifts

To shift from a fixed mindset to a growth mindset, individuals can practice several strategies that enhance adaptability.

- **Practicing Self-Reflection and Mindfulness:** Mindfulness encourages present-moment awareness, which can reduce the fear of uncertainty and help individuals remain grounded during changes (Kabat-Zinn, 2003). Regular self-reflection allows individuals to evaluate their responses to change and identify areas for growth.

• **Setting Incremental Goals to Build Confidence:** Setting small, achievable goals helps build confidence and reinforces a growth mindset. Each small success demonstrates that progress is possible, even in the face of challenges. This approach also reduces overwhelming feelings, making change more manageable (Locke & Latham, 2002).

• **Embracing Lifelong Learning:** Lifelong learning is essential for adaptability. Individuals become more flexible and open to change by continuously seeking new knowledge and skills. This mindset promotes curiosity and encourages personal development, vital for resilience in a fast-paced world (Gurteen, 2012).

REAL-LIFE EXAMPLES

• **An Entrepreneur Pivoting Their Business Model:** Sarah, a small business owner, faced significant challenges during the COVID-19 pandemic. When her physical store closed, she quickly transitioned to an online platform. Embracing this change allowed her business to survive and thrive in a new environment. Her willingness to learn digital marketing skills and embrace e-commerce demonstrated the power of adaptability in times of crisis (Krishnan & Scullion, 2021).

• **A Professional Navigating a Career Change:** After years in a corporate role, John found himself at a crossroads when his company was restructured. Rather than seeing this as a setback, he used the opportunity to retrain in a new field—data analytics. His ability to embrace lifelong learning and pivot his career path helped him find success in an emerging industry (Adams, 2020).

Developing Problem-Solving Skills

Adaptability is closely linked to problem-solving abilities. When faced with challenges, individuals who can assess the situation, weigh options, and develop solutions are better equipped to navigate change.

• **Importance of Problem-Solving**: Effective problem-solving reduces uncertainty by providing clarity and direction. It enhances decision-making capabilities and lowers the stress associated with unresolved challenges. Studies have shown that individuals with strong problem-solving skills are more adaptable and less likely to experience anxiety during changes (Heppner & Petersen, 1982).

Problem-Solving Frameworks

Several frameworks can help individuals develop and refine their problem-solving skills, enhancing their ability to adapt to new situations.

• **The 5 Whys Technique**: This simple yet powerful technique involves asking "why" five times to get to the root cause of a problem. By identifying the underlying issue, individuals can develop more effective solutions (Serrat, 2017).

• **SWOT Analysis**: This framework helps individuals assess the strengths, weaknesses, opportunities, and threats associated with a situation. By analyzing these factors, they can make informed decisions and develop strategies to navigate challenges (Pickton & Wright, 1998).

• **The PDCA Cycle (Plan, Do, Check, Act)**: The PDCA cycle is a continuous improvement method that encourages individuals to plan a solution, implement it, check the results, and adjust as needed. This iterative process allows for ongoing adaptation and improvement (Deming, 1986).

Practical Exercises

To build problem-solving skills, try the following exercises:

• **Brainstorming Sessions**: Regular brainstorming helps develop creativity and flexibility in thinking. Individuals can explore different perspectives and approaches by generating multiple solutions to a problem (Osborn, 1957).

• **Scenario Planning:** This technique involves imagining different future scenarios and planning responses to each one. By anticipating potential challenges, individuals can develop adaptable strategies and reduce uncertainty (Schoemaker, 1995).

REAL-LIFE APPLICATIONS

• **A Project Manager Resolving Team Conflicts:** When tensions arose within her team, a project manager used the 5 Whys technique to uncover the root cause of the conflict. She resolved the dispute by addressing the underlying issue—miscommunication regarding roles and responsibilities—and improved team collaboration (Heifetz & Linsky, 2002).

• **An Individual Managing Personal Financial Challenges:** After experiencing job loss, Jane used SWOT analysis to assess her strengths (financial planning skills), weaknesses (limited savings), opportunities (freelance work), and threats (debt). This framework helped her develop a plan to stabilize her finances and pursue new income opportunities (Kiyosaki, 1997).

The Role of Flexibility in Resilience

Flexibility is the ability to adjust plans and strategies in response to changing circumstances. It is a critical component of resilience, allowing individuals to remain open to new possibilities and navigate unexpected challenges.

• **Defining Flexibility:** Flexibility involves a willingness to alter one's approach and explore alternative solutions when faced with obstacles. It requires an open mind and letting go of rigid expectations (Block, 2002).

• **Benefits of Flexibility:** Flexibility enhances creativity, as individuals are more likely to consider innovative solutions when they are open to change. It also reduces stress, as flexible individuals are less likely to feel frustrated when things don't go according to plan (Bonanno, 2004).

Developing Flexibility

To become more flexible, individuals can practice the following strategies:

• **Practicing Active Listening and Empathy:** Flexibility requires considering other perspectives. By actively listening to others and practicing empathy, individuals can expand their understanding and develop more adaptable solutions (Rogers, 1957).

• **Trying New Experiences and Stepping Out of Comfort Zones:** Engaging in new activities and experiences challenges existing assumptions and encourages flexibility. Whether learning a new skill or traveling to a different country, stepping out of your comfort zone fosters adaptability (Bennis & Thomas, 2002).

• **Setting Aside Time for Reflection and Adjustment:** Regularly reflecting on experiences and adjusting plans is essential for flexibility. This practice allows individuals to learn from their experiences and make necessary course corrections (Kolb, 1984).

Real-Life Examples

• **A Teacher Adapting Lesson Plans to Remote Learning:** Teachers worldwide had to adapt to online education quickly during the pandemic. One teacher embraced this change by developing creative ways to engage students remotely, using technology to facilitate interactive lessons and maintain connection (Carrillo & Flores, 2020).

• **A Traveler Adjusting to Unexpected Changes in Plans:** When a flight was canceled due to weather, a traveler used the opportunity to explore a new city during the layover. Her flexibility allowed her to enjoy the unexpected detour rather than viewing it as an inconvenience (Adams, 2020).

Adapting to New Professional Challenges

The modern professional world is ever-changing. Professionals who can navigate industry changes, technological advancements, and shifting company cultures are more likely to experience career growth and job satisfaction. Adaptability in the workplace fosters innovation, enhances problem-solving abilities, and reduces stress as individuals learn to embrace new responsibilities and technologies rather than resist them (Friedman & Krackhardt, 2017).

IDENTIFYING **Professional Challenges**

Some standard professional challenges that require adaptability include:

- **Changes in Job Roles and Responsibilities:** Job roles often shift as companies evolve. This shifting landscape can require individuals to learn new skills or take on additional responsibilities.

- **Shifts in Company Culture or Leadership:** Leadership transitions or changes in company values can create uncertainty. Adapting to these shifts can be critical for career advancement and workplace harmony (Kotter, 2012).

STRATEGIES FOR PROFESSIONAL **Adaptability**

To become more adaptable at work, consider these actionable steps:

- **Continuous Learning and Skill Development:** The professional world constantly changes, and keeping up requires lifelong learning. Pursue new certifications, attend industry conferences, or take online courses to stay updated on emerging trends and technologies (Gurteen, 2012).

- **Building a Diverse Professional Network:** A strong network can provide support and guidance during periods of change. Networking with professionals from various fields also exposes you to new ideas and perspectives, helping you adapt to different challenges (Kuhn, 2000).

• **Seeking Feedback and Mentoring**: Constructive feedback is a valuable tool for growth. Regularly seek feedback from supervisors and peers, and consider finding a mentor who can help guide you through professional transitions (Clutterbuck, 2004).

SUCCESS STORIES

• **A Marketing Professional Learning New Digital Tools**: Joyce, a marketing professional, realized that her traditional marketing skills were becoming outdated in the digital age. Rather than resisting the change, she enrolled in online courses to learn digital marketing techniques, such as SEO and social media strategy. Her adaptability allowed her to stay competitive and achieve career growth (Kim, 2020).

• **An Employee Transitioning to a Leadership Role**: George faced new responsibilities and challenges when he was promoted to a managerial position. He sought mentorship from an experienced leader and attended leadership workshops to develop the necessary skills. By embracing the learning process, George successfully transitioned into his new role (Adams, 2020).

Strategies for Personal Transitions

Personal transitions, like moving to a new city, changing careers, or managing health issues, can be emotionally challenging. Developing adaptability during these transitions is critical to maintaining resilience.

• **Understanding Personal Transitions**: Personal transitions often involve significant emotional adjustment. These changes require emotional resilience and adaptability, whether starting over after a loss or adjusting to a new relationship dynamic (Schlossberg, 1981).

· · ·

Planning for Transitions

Planning for personal transitions can reduce the emotional impact and provide a sense of control. Consider the following strategies:

- **Creating a Transition Plan with Clear Goals:** When facing a significant life transition, developing a plan outlining your goals and steps for achieving them is helpful. For example, if you're moving to a new city, your plan might include securing housing, finding a job, and establishing social connections.

- **Seeking Support from Family and Friends:** Support from loved ones can ease the stress of transitions. Whether it's practical help or emotional encouragement, staying connected with your support system is essential for navigating change (Cutrona & Russell, 1990).

- **Practicing Self-Care During Transitions:** Self-care practices like exercise, meditation, and adequate rest are crucial for managing stress during times of change. They also help maintain physical and emotional well-being (Segerstrom & Miller, 2004).

Coping with Uncertainty

Change often brings uncertainty, which can cause anxiety. Here are some techniques for handling uncertainty:

- **Building a Routine to Maintain Stability:** Establishing a daily routine can provide structure and a sense of normalcy during transitions. A routine is essential when everything else feels uncertain.

- **Focusing on What Can Be Controlled:** Rather than dwelling on aspects of the transition outside your control, focus on what you can influence. For example, if you're dealing with a health issue, adopt healthy habits supporting your well-being (Taylor et al., 2000).

Real-Life Examples

- **Someone Starting Over After a Significant Loss:** After the death of her spouse, Linda faced the daunting task of rebuilding her life. She sought support from a grief counseling group and gradually set small goals, such as volunteering and reconnecting with friends. Over time, Linda found new meaning and purpose through these steps (Neimeyer, 2001).

• **A Person Relocating to a New City and Building a New Life:** When he moved to a new city for a job, Adam initially felt overwhelmed by the unfamiliar environment. To adapt, he created a detailed transition plan, which included joining local clubs and attending community events. This approach helped him build a social network and adjust to his new surroundings (Adams, 2020).

Building Resilience in a Rapidly Changing World

The pace of change in today's world—driven by technological advancements, globalization, and environmental challenges—requires individuals to be highly adaptable. Those who can quickly adjust to new realities are likelier to thrive.

Rapid technological advancements and globalization have transformed industries, creating new opportunities and significant challenges. Environmental issues and societal shifts have further contributed to the uncertainty in today's world (Susskind & Susskind, 2015).

STAYING Informed and Prepared

Staying informed about industry trends and societal changes is critical for preparing for the future.

• **Keeping Up with Industry Trends and News:** To remain competitive and adaptable, individuals should regularly update their knowledge by reading industry publications, attending webinars, or following thought leaders in their field (Kuhn, 2000).

• **Developing Contingency Plans:** Preparing for different scenarios by creating contingency plans can reduce anxiety and uncertainty. These plans provide a roadmap for responding to potential challenges in your career or personal life (Schoemaker, 1995).

. . .

INNOVATIVE THINKING **and Adaptation**

Fostering innovative thinking is essential for adapting to change.

• **Encouraging a Culture of Innovation:** In professional settings, encouraging innovation can create a more adaptable work environment. Steps might involve promoting creative problem-solving, welcoming diverse perspectives, and rewarding innovative ideas (Amabile, 1996).

• **Experimenting with New Ideas and Approaches:** Trying new approaches can foster adaptability in business or personal life. By experimenting with different methods and being open to failure, individuals can learn what works and refine their strategies over time (Dweck, 2006).

INSPIRATIONAL STORIES

• **A Company Pivoting Its Business Model During a Crisis:** During the COVID-19 pandemic, many businesses had to pivot to survive. One restaurant chain embraced change by transitioning to a meal delivery service and offering virtual cooking classes. This adaptability allowed the business to thrive in a challenging environment (Krishnan & Scullion, 2021).

• **An Individual Leveraging Technology for Personal Growth:** Maria, a working mother, used technology to continue her education during the pandemic. She enrolled in online courses and earned a new certification, leading to a work promotion. Her ability to adapt and leverage digital tools exemplifies resilience in a rapidly changing world (Adams, 2020).

Biblical Example: Esther's Courage and Adaptability in the Face of Danger

The story of Esther is one of remarkable courage and adaptability. Esther, a Jewish woman, found herself in a foreign land and unexpectedly became the queen of Persia. When a decree was issued to annihilate all the Jews in the kingdom, Esther faced a life-changing decision. Her cousin Mordecai urged her to intervene with King Xerxes, but doing so could have cost her life, as approaching the king without being summoned was punishable by death.

Despite her fears, Esther adapted to the complex political environment. She didn't act impulsively; instead, she fasted and prayed for three days, seeking wisdom and strength from God. Then, using strategic thinking, Esther invited the king and Haman to a series of banquets, slowly revealing her true identity and the plot against her people (Esther 4:13-16; Esther 7:1-10). Through her wisdom and flexibility, Esther saved the Jewish people from destruction.

Esther's ability to navigate the dangerous waters of the Persian court shows the importance of adaptability in high-pressure situations. Her story shows how faith, courage, and careful strategy can lead to successful outcomes even in dire circumstances. Esther's adaptability helped her turn a potential catastrophe into a triumph, protecting her people and securing their future.

Her example encourages us to remain flexible and courageous in the face of uncertainty, to use wisdom when making decisions, and to trust in God's plan when facing adversity. Like Esther, we can embrace adaptability to overcome challenges and bring about meaningful change.

REFERENCES

Adams, S. (2020). *Navigating Change in Career and Life*. Harper-Collins.

Bennis, W., & Thomas, R. J. (2002). *Geeks and Geezers: How Era, Values, and Defining Moments Shape Leaders*. Harvard Business Review Press.

Bonanno, G. A. (2004). Loss, trauma, and human resilience: Have we underestimated the human capacity to thrive after extremely aversive events? *American Psychologist, 59*(1), 20-28.

Carrillo, C., & Flores, M. A. (2020). COVID-19 and educational change: How teachers adapted to online learning. *European Journal of Teacher Education, 43*(4), 442-456.

Cutrona, C. E., & Russell, D. W. (1990). Type of social support and specific stress: Toward a theory of optimal matching. In I. G. Sarason, B. R. Sarason, & G. R. Pierce (Eds.), *Social support: An interactional view* (pp. 319–366). Wiley.

Deming, W. E. (1986). *Out of the Crisis*. MIT Press.

Dweck, C. S. (2006). *Mindset: The New Psychology of Success*. Random House.

Friedman, L. W., & Krackhardt, D. (2017). The impact of organizational flexibility on performance. *Organization Science, 20*(1), 10-23.

Gurteen, D. (2012). Knowledge, innovation, and adaptability: How knowledge management helps companies innovate and stay flexible. *The Journal of Information and Knowledge Management Systems, 42*(3), 348-359.

Heifetz, R. A., & Linsky, M. (2002). *Leadership on the Line: Staying Alive Through the Dangers of Leading*. Harvard Business Review Press.

Heppner, P. P., & Petersen, C. H. (1982). The development and implications of a personal problem-solving inventory. *Journal of Counseling Psychology, 29*(1), 66-75.

Kabat-Zinn, J. (2003). Mindfulness-based interventions in context: Past, present, and future. *Clinical Psychology: Science and Practice, 10*(2), 144-156.

Kiyosaki, R. T. (1997). *Rich Dad Poor Dad: What the Rich Teach Their Kids About Money That the Poor and Middle Class Do Not!*. Warner Books.

Kotter, J. P. (2012). *Leading Change*. Harvard Business Review Press.

Krishnan, T., & Scullion, D. (2021). *Business Transformation During Crisis: Lessons from the COVID-19 Pandemic*. Routledge.

Locke, E. A., & Latham, G. P. (2002). Building a practically useful theory of goal setting and task motivation: A 35-year odyssey. *American Psychologist, 57*(9), 705-717.

Neimeyer, R. A. (2001). *Meaning Reconstruction and the Experience of Loss*. American Psychological Association.

Osborn, A. F. (1957). *Applied Imagination: Principles and Procedures of Creative Problem-Solving*. Scribner.

Pickton, D. W., & Wright, S. (1998). What's SWOT in strategic analysis? *Strategic Change, 7*(2), 101-109.

Rogers, C. R. (1957). The necessary and sufficient conditions of therapeutic personality change. *Journal of Consulting Psychology, 21*(2), 95-103.

Schoemaker, P. J. (1995). Scenario planning: A tool for strategic thinking. *MIT Sloan Management Review, 36*(2), 25-40.

Segerstrom, S. C., & Miller, G. E. (2004). Psychological stress and the human immune system: A meta-analytic study of 30 years of inquiry. *Psychological Bulletin, 130*(4), 601-630.

Serrat, O. (2017). The five whys technique. In *Knowledge Solutions: Tools, Methods, and Approaches to Drive Organizational Performance* (pp. 307-310). Springer.

Susskind, R., & Susskind, D. (2015). *The Future of the Professions: How Technology Will Transform the Work of Human Experts*. Oxford University Press.

Taylor, S. E., Kemeny, M. E., Reed, G. M., Bower, J. E., & Gruenewald, T. L. (2000). Psychological resources, positive illusions, and health. *American Psychologist, 55*(1), 99-109.

Yeager, D. S., & Dweck, C. S. (2012). Mindsets that promote resilience: When students believe that personal characteristics can be developed. *Educational Psychologist, 47*(4), 302-314.

7

HEALTH AND WELLNESS AS A FOUNDATION FOR RESILIENCE

Physical health and mental well-being are inseparable aspects of human resilience. How we care for our bodies—through exercise, diet, and stress-relief practices—directly impacts our capacity to face challenges and bounce back from adversity. This chapter explores the critical role of health and wellness in building resilience, providing practical advice for integrating healthy habits into daily life.

Quick Workout Routines for Busy Schedules

Finding time for exercise can be challenging in the modern world, but regular physical activity is essential for mental and emotional resilience.

• **Importance of Physical Activity:** Regular exercise has been shown to reduce stress hormones like cortisol while increasing the production of endorphins, improving mood, and promoting well-being (Hillman et al., 2008). Studies have consistently demonstrated the link between physical health and mental well-being, with physical activity contributing to enhanced cognitive function and emotional regulation (Fox, 1999).

• **Efficient Workouts:** For those with busy schedules, high-intensity interval training (HIIT) offers an effective way to fit exercise into short bursts of time. HIIT routines can be completed in as little as 10 minutes and provide significant cardiovascular benefits. Simple bodyweight exercises, like push-ups, squats, and lunges, can also be done quickly at home or during short breaks. For office workers, desk exercises, such as chair squats or seated leg raises, can help maintain mobility and reduce the strain of prolonged sitting (Tremblay et al., 2010).

• **Incorporating Exercise into Daily Life:** Physical activity can be easily integrated into everyday routines besides formal workouts. Walking or biking to work, taking short breaks for movement during the day, or using stairs instead of elevators are all simple ways to stay active without dedicating significant amounts of time. Regular movement helps prevent the buildup of stress and supports long-term health (Warburton et al., 2006).

Real-Life Examples

• **A Parent Balancing Exercise with Family Responsibilities:** Sarah, a working mother of two, found it challenging to carve out time for fitness. Instead of long gym sessions, she began incorporating quick 10-minute workouts at home between her children's activities. This change allowed her to stay fit without sacrificing family time.

• **A Professional Fitting Workouts into a Demanding Job Schedule:** Michael, a corporate executive, found that his long hours left little time for self-care. To address this, he began taking short exercise breaks during his workday, using a standing desk, and performing desk exercises. This practice improved his energy levels and helped him manage stress more effectively.

Balanced Meal Planning for Mental Clarity

Nutrition plays a crucial role in maintaining mental clarity and emotional balance. A well-balanced diet provides the nutrients necessary for optimal brain function and supports resilience.

• **Link Between Diet and Mental Health:** The brain requires a steady supply of nutrients to function correctly. A diet rich in essential nutrients, such as omega-3 fatty acids, antioxidants, and vitamins, supports cognitive function and helps regulate mood. Research has shown that fluctuations in blood sugar levels, often caused by processed foods and simple carbohydrates, can lead to irritability, fatigue, and mood swings (Benton & Donohoe, 1999).

• **Components of a Balanced Diet**: A balanced diet should include a mix of proteins, fats, carbohydrates, and micronutrients like vitamins and minerals. For mental clarity, it is essential to prioritize foods that provide long-lasting energy, such as whole grains, lean proteins, and healthy fats. Hydration is equally crucial; drinking enough water throughout the day ensures the brain functions optimally (Armstrong et al., 2012).

• **Meal Planning Tips**: Meal prep can simplify maintaining a healthy diet. Preparing meals beforehand allows for thoughtful planning, ensuring each meal is balanced and nutritious. Aim to create a balanced plate with lean protein, whole grains, and plenty of fruits and vegetables. Healthy snacks, such as nuts, yogurt, or fruit, can boost energy between meals.

Scientific Evidence

• **Studies on the Mediterranean Diet**: Research has demonstrated that the Mediterranean diet, rich in fruits, vegetables, whole grains, and healthy fats, is associated with better mental health outcomes and reduced risks of depression and anxiety (Sánchez-Villegas et al., 2009).

• **The Role of Omega-3 Fatty Acids**: Omega-3s, found in foods like fatty fish, walnuts, and flaxseeds, play a crucial role in brain health and have been linked to improved mood regulation. Studies suggest that omega-3 supplements may help reduce symptoms of depression (Freeman et al., 2006).

Stress-Relief Activities for Everyday Life

Chronic stress can have severe consequences for both physical and mental health. Engaging in regular stress-relief activities is essential for maintaining resilience.

• **Importance of Stress Relief**: Stress activates the body's fight-or-flight response, releasing cortisol and other stress hormones. While short bursts of stress can be motivating, chronic stress wears down the body and mind, contributing to a host of health issues, including cardiovascular disease and mental health disorders (McEwen, 1998). Stress-relief activities help mitigate these effects, promoting overall well-being and resilience.

• **Types of Stress-Relief Activities:** There are many ways to relieve stress, and the best methods resonate with the individual. Hobbies such as gardening, painting, or knitting provide a creative outlet for relaxation. Relaxation techniques, such as progressive muscle relaxation and deep breathing, can also be incorporated into daily life. Physical activities like yoga and tai chi are excellent for relieving stress while promoting physical health (Janssen et al., 2010).

• **Creating a Stress-Relief Routine:** A regular stress-relief routine is vital to ensuring that relaxation becomes a priority. Scheduling time for relaxation activities, even in small increments, ensures they are part of the daily routine. Combining stress-relief activities with other tasks—like listening to music while cooking or stretching before bed—can make it easier to integrate relaxation into busy lives.

Real-Life Examples

• **A Busy Executive Practicing Yoga for Stress Management:** Jennifer, a high-powered executive, found that stress negatively affected her productivity and well-being. She began incorporating yoga into her morning routine, which helped her manage stress and improve her focus at work.

• **A Student Using Creative Hobbies to Unwind:** Daniel, a college student, struggled with the pressures of exams and deadlines. He found relief by dedicating time each evening to painting, which allowed him to relax and recharge.

The Connection Between Physical and Mental Health

There is a well-established connection between physical health and mental resilience. When we prioritize our physical well-being, our mental health benefits as well.

• **Explaining the Connection:** Physical and mental health are intricately linked in a bidirectional relationship. Physical conditions, such as chronic pain or illness, can affect mental health by contributing to feelings of frustration, hopelessness, or depression. Conversely, mental health disorders can manifest physically, leading to symptoms such as fatigue or insomnia (Prince et al., 2007).

- **Benefits of Physical Health for Mental Resilience:** Good physical health supports mental resilience by improving sleep quality, enhancing cognitive function, and boosting energy levels. Exercise, for example, has been shown to reduce symptoms of depression and anxiety while improving mood and cognitive function (Dishman et al., 2006).

- **Holistic Health Approaches:** Holistic approaches to health, such as integrative medicine and mind-body practices like yoga and tai chi, address physical and mental well-being. These practices emphasize balance and harmony within the body, promoting overall health and resilience (Lee et al., 2004).

Scientific Research

- **Physical Activity and Depression:** Studies show that regular physical activity can significantly reduce symptoms of depression and anxiety. Exercise stimulates the release of neurotransmitters like serotonin and dopamine, which play a role in mood regulation (Blumenthal et al., 1999).

- **The Mental Health Benefits of Maintaining a Healthy Weight:** Research also indicates that maintaining a healthy weight through diet and exercise reduces the risk of mental health disorders, particularly depression (Simon et al., 2006).

Integrating Wellness Practices into Daily Routine

Consistency is critical to building resilience through health and wellness practices. Daily routines incorporating wellness strategies can lay the foundation for long-term mental and physical resilience.

- **Importance of Daily Wellness Practices:** Small, consistent wellness practices create a foundation for sustained health. Whether drinking enough water, taking short walks, or practicing Mindfulness, these actions accumulate over time, helping build resilience (Mayo Clinic, 2019).

• **Types of Wellness Practices:** Wellness practices can take many forms, including Mindfulness meditation, healthy eating habits, and regular physical activity. Integrating these practices into daily life helps ensure that they become sustainable habits.

• **Developing a Wellness Routine:** A successful wellness routine is realistic and adaptable. Start with small, manageable goals, track progress, and adjust as needed to ensure long-term success. For example, setting a goal to meditate for five minutes daily is more achievable and sustainable than immediately attempting a more extended session.

Real-Life Examples

• **A Professional Balancing Work and Wellness Routines:** Lisa, a lawyer, found it challenging to maintain a healthy lifestyle while juggling a demanding job. She began incorporating short Mindfulness breaks and stretching exercises into her day, which improved her focus and energy.

• **A Family Incorporating Wellness Practices into Daily Life:** The Miller family committed to wellness by going on evening walks together after dinner. They also introduced healthier meal options, focusing on balanced plates with more vegetables, whole grains, and lean proteins. These small, consistent steps helped the family bond while improving their health and well-being.

The Impact of Regular Exercise on Resilience

Regular exercise is one of the most effective ways to enhance physical and mental resilience. Consistent physical activity improves physical health and profoundly affects emotional and psychological well-being.

• **Benefits of Regular Exercise:** Regular physical activity has been shown to enhance mood, reduce symptoms of anxiety and depression, and increase overall energy levels. Exercise's mental health benefits are partly due to the release of endorphins, which improve mood and create a sense of well-being (Fox, 1999). Exercise also improves sleep quality, closely linked to mental resilience (Driver & Taylor, 2000).

• **Types of Exercises That Boost Resilience:** Various exercises can contribute to building resilience. Cardiovascular exercises like running or cycling help improve endurance and overall heart health. Strength training, including weight lifting and resistance band exercises, strengthens muscles and bones, providing a solid physical foundation. Flexibility exercises, like yoga and stretching, improve range of motion and help reduce the risk of injury (Warburton et al., 2006).

• **Creating an Exercise Routine:** A sustainable exercise routine is essential to maintaining consistency. Start by setting specific fitness goals—whether walking 30 minutes a day or lifting weights three times a week—and find activities that are enjoyable and suited to your lifestyle. Incorporating variety into your routine can help prevent boredom and reduce the risk of overuse injuries. For example, balancing cardio, strength training, and flexibility exercises can create a balanced fitness plan.

Scientific Evidence

• **Mental Health Benefits of Physical Activity:** Numerous studies have shown the positive effects of regular exercise on mental health. For instance, a study by Blumenthal et al. (1999) demonstrated that exercise is as effective as medication in treating depression, especially for individuals with mild to moderate symptoms.

• **Long-Term Effects of Consistent Exercise on Stress Reduction:** Regular physical activity has also been shown to lower cortisol levels, the hormone associated with stress. Over time, consistent exercise contributes to long-term stress management, helping individuals cope more effectively with life's challenges (Hillman et al., 2008).

Biblical Example: Daniel's Physical and Spiritual Discipline

In the Book of Daniel, we find a compelling story highlighting the connection between physical health, spiritual resilience, and adaptability. Daniel and other young men of Judah were taken captive and brought to Babylon to serve in King Nebuchadnezzar's court. Upon arrival, they were offered the rich food and wine from the king's table. However, Daniel chose not to defile himself with these indulgences and requested permission to eat only vegetables and drink water (Daniel 1:8-16).

Daniel's decision to maintain a simple, nutritious diet, rooted in his faith and discipline, set him apart. After ten days, Daniel and his companions were healthier and more physically fit than those who partook of the royal delicacies. Beyond the physical benefits, this act of discipline strengthened Daniel's spiritual resilience. His commitment to a healthy physical and spiritual lifestyle empowered him to face the challenges and trials that would come later in his life, including his remarkable survival in the lion's den.

Daniel's story illustrates the importance of prioritizing health and discipline in facing external pressures. It shows that caring for our physical well-being enhances our resilience and supports our spiritual strength. By maintaining his diet and devotion to God, Daniel exemplified how physical and spiritual practices work to build enduring resilience.

References

Armstrong, L. E., Ganio, M. S., Klau, J. F., Johnson, E. C., Casa, D. J., & Maresh, C. M. (2012). Hydration and cognitive function in healthy adults. *Nutrition Reviews, 70*(2), S99-S109.

Benton, D., & Donohoe, R. T. (1999). The effects of nutrients on mood. *Public Health Nutrition, 2*(3A), 403-409.

Blumenthal, J. A., Babyak, M. A., Doraiswamy, P. M., Watkins, L., Hoffman, B. M., Barbour, K. A., ... & Sherwood, A. (1999). Exercise and pharmacotherapy in the treatment of major depressive disorder. *Psychosomatic Medicine, 61*(5), 666–675.

Dishman, R. K., Berthoud, H. R., Booth, F. W., Cotman, C. W., Edgerton, V. R., Fleshner, M. R., ... & Zigmond, M. J. (2006). Neurobiology of exercise. *Obesity, 14*(3), 345–356.

Driver, H. S., & Taylor, S. R. (2000). Exercise and sleep. *Sleep Medicine Reviews, 4*(4), 387-402.

Fox, K. R. (1999). The influence of physical activity on mental well-being. *Public Health Nutrition, 2*(3A), pp. 411–418.

Freeman, M. P., Hibbeln, J. R., Wisner, K. L., Davis, J. M., Mischoulon, D., Peet, M., ... & Stoll, A. L. (2006). Omega-3 fatty acids: Evidence basis for treatment and future research in psychiatry. *Journal of Clinical Psychiatry, 67*(12), 1954-1967.

Hillman, C. H., Erickson, K. I., & Kramer, A. F. (2008). Be smart, exercise your heart: Exercise effects on brain and cognition. *Nature Reviews Neuroscience, 9*(1), 58-65.

Janssen, M., Heerkens, Y., Kuijer, W., van der Heijden, B., & Engels, J. (2010). Effects of Mindfulness-based stress reduction on employees' mental health: A systematic review. *PloS One, 15*(12), e0243185.

McEwen, B. S. (1998). Protective and damaging effects of stress mediators. *New England Journal of Medicine, 338*(3), 171-179.

Sánchez-Villegas, A., Martínez-González, M. Á., Estruch, R., Salas-Salvadó, J., Corella, D., Covas, M. I., ... & Ros, E. (2009). Mediterranean diet and depression: the PREDIMED randomized trial. *BMC Medicine, 11*(1), 125-135.

Simon, G. E., Von Korff, M., Saunders, K., Miglioretti, D. L., Crane, P. K., van Belle, G., & Kessler, R. C. (2006). Association between obesity and psychiatric disorders in the US adult population. *Archives of General Psychiatry, 63*(7), 824-830.

Tremblay, M. S., Colley, R. C., Saunders, T. J., Healy, G. N., & Owen, N. (2010). Physiological and health implications of a sedentary lifestyle. *Applied Physiology, Nutrition, and Metabolism, 35*(6), 725–740.

Warburton, D. E., Nicol, C. W., & Bredin, S. S. (2006). Health benefits of physical activity: the evidence. *Canadian Medical Association Journal, 174*(6), 801-809.

8

LONG-TERM GROWTH AND CONTINUOUS IMPROVEMENT

Long-term resilience develops through continuous growth, learning, and self-improvement. Embracing a growth mindset, engaging in lifelong learning, and setting meaningful goals are vital to sustaining resilience over time. This chapter explores strategies for long-term growth and how to build a legacy of resilience that can inspire and support future generations.

Developing a Growth Mindset

A growth mindset is the belief that abilities and intelligence develop through effort, learning, and perseverance. This empowering mindset is not just crucial for long-term resilience, but it also encourages adaptability and a willingness to embrace challenges, inspiring you to push your boundaries and achieve more.

- **Understanding the Growth Mindset:** Unlike a fixed mindset, where individuals believe their abilities are static, a growth mindset sees challenges as opportunities for personal growth (Dweck, 2006). People with a growth mindset are more likely to take risks, learn from mistakes, and persist when facing difficulties.
- **Characteristics of a Growth Mindset:**

o   **Adaptability**: The ability to adjust to new situations and challenges.

o   **Openness to Learning**: A desire to learn new skills and improve existing ones.

o **Resilience**: The willingness to persist in the face of setbacks.

• **Benefits of a Growth Mindset**:

o **Increased Adaptability**: A growth mindset fosters openness to new experiences and encourages individuals to explore unfamiliar paths.

o **Enhanced Problem-Solving Abilities**: When challenges arise, those with a growth mindset are more likely to engage in creative problem-solving rather than feeling defeated.

Cultivating a Growth Mindset

Developing a growth mindset requires intentional effort and practice. Here are a few strategies for cultivating this mindset:

• **Embracing Challenges**: Viewing challenges as growth opportunities rather than obstacles is essential. Instead of avoiding demanding tasks, approach them as learning experiences.

• **Viewing Effort as the Path to Mastery**: Effort is not a sign of weakness but rather the route to achieving excellence. Accept that mastery requires time and perseverance.

• **Learning from Criticism and Feedback**: Constructive feedback is a powerful tool for growth. Instead of taking criticism personally, use it as an opportunity to improve.

Real-Life Applications

• **An Athlete Overcoming Setbacks to Achieve Success**: Consider the story of Michael Jordan, one of the greatest basketball players ever. Jordan was cut from his high school basketball team early in his career. However, he used this setback as motivation to work harder, eventually becoming an NBA legend (Lazenby, 2014).

• **An Entrepreneur Embracing Failure as a Stepping Stone**:

Sarah Blakely, founder of Spanx, attributes much of her success to the lessons she learned from failure. She embraced challenges, learned from mistakes, and continued to innovate until her business became a multi-billion-dollar company (Blakely, 2018).

Continuous Learning: The Key to Long-Term Success

Continuous learning is not just a good practice but a necessity for resilience and long-term success. In a constantly evolving world, keeping skills and knowledge up-to-date is crucial for personal and professional growth.

- **Importance of Lifelong Learning**: Lifelong learning enhances cognitive abilities, flexibility, and adaptability. It helps individuals stay relevant in their careers and prepares them to face new challenges confidently (Kolb, 2014).

TYPES OF LEARNING Opportunities

- **Formal Education**: Formal education provides structured learning environments and deep knowledge in specific areas.
- **Informal Learning**: Workshops, online courses, and webinars are great avenues for acquiring new skills. Informal learning is more flexible and allows individuals to learn at their own pace.
- **Experiential Learning**: Internships, volunteer work, and hands-on experiences offer practical knowledge that is often more applicable than theoretical learning. These opportunities allow for real-world application and problem-solving (Kolb, 2014).

CREATING a Learning Plan

Developing a personalized learning plan can guide long-term growth and continuous improvement. The steps include:

- **Identifying Areas for Growth**: Reflect on personal and professional goals and identify the skills or knowledge needed to achieve them.

- **Setting Specific Learning Goals:** Define clear and measurable objectives to guide learning.
- **Finding Resources and Opportunities:** Research educational programs, online courses, or mentorship opportunities that align with your goals.

Success Stories

- **A Professional Advancing Their Career Through Ongoing Education:** Jessica, a marketing executive, enrolled in digital marketing courses to stay competitive. She continuously updated her skills and won a leadership role within her company.
- **A Hobbyist Turning Their Passion into Expertise:** John, a weekend woodworker, took online carpentry courses and began offering custom furniture services. His continuous learning transformed a hobby into a successful side business.

Setting Long-Term Resilience Goals

Setting meaningful, long-term goals is essential for sustained growth and resilience. These clear goals not only provide direction and motivation but also a sense of purpose, helping you stay committed to your personal and professional development journey.

- **Importance of Long-Term Goals:** Long-term goals provide a sense of purpose and clarity. They encourage sustained effort and commitment necessary for personal growth and resilience (Locke & Latham, 2002).

Creating SMART Long-Term Goals

Practical long-term goals follow the SMART framework:

- **Specific:** Clearly define the goal. For example, "Build a Mindfulness practice" is specific, while "Improve mental health" is vague.
- **Measurable:** Establish criteria to track progress, such as "Practice Mindfulness for 10 minutes daily."

- **Achievable:** Ensure the goal is realistic and within reach.
- **Relevant:** Align the goal with personal values and aspirations.
- **Time-bound:** Set a timeline for achieving the goal, such as "Incorporate Mindfulness daily for the next six months."

Examples of Long-Term Goals

- **Personal Development:** "Build a daily Mindfulness practice over the next year."
- **Career Advancement:** "Achieve a leadership position within five years."

Strategies for Staying Committed

- **Reviewing and Adjusting Goals:** Regularly assess progress and adjust goals as needed. Flexibility is critical to long-term success.
- **Seeking Support and Accountability:** To stay on track, share your goals with a mentor or accountability partner.
- **Celebrating Milestones:** Recognize and celebrate achievements to maintain motivation.

Monitoring Progress and Adjusting Strategies

Tracking progress is essential for staying focused on long-term goals and adapting to any obstacles along the way.

- **Tracking Progress:** Use tools like journals, planners, or digital apps to monitor achievements and setbacks. Regularly reflecting on progress helps maintain motivation and focus.

Tools for Monitoring

- **Journals or Planners:** Writing down goals and reflecting on progress helps keep track of personal growth.
- **Digital Apps:** Apps like Trello, Asana, or Google Keep can help track tasks and goals.
- **Regular Self-Assessments:** Periodically evaluating strengths and areas for improvement is essential for adjusting strategies.

.   .   .

Adjusting Strategies

Sometimes, strategies need to be adapted to meet changing circumstances. Analyze what's working, make necessary changes, and stay flexible in your approach to long-term growth.

Real-Life Examples

• **A Student Adapting Study Methods**: Maria struggled with her study routine and grades. She improved her academic performance by using self-assessments and adjusting her study habits.

• **A Professional Refining Their Career Path**: After receiving feedback, Daniel, a project manager, adjusted his approach to leadership and communication, resulting in improved team dynamics.

Inspirational Stories of Lifelong Resilience

Real-life stories of resilience are commanding examples of the human capacity to grow, adapt, and persevere through challenges.

• **A Survivor Overcoming Significant Adversity**: Consider the story of Nelson Mandela, who spent 27 years in prison yet emerged with a vision for a better South Africa. His perseverance and resilience in adversity continue to inspire people worldwide (Mandela, 1994).

• **An Innovator Disrupting an Industry**: Elon Musk's journey from struggling startups to leading space exploration and electric vehicles demonstrates the power of resilience and continuous learning in achieving long-term success (Vance, 2015).

• **A Community Leader Fostering Resilience in Others**: Malala Yousafzai's advocacy for girls' education in the face of opposition exemplifies resilience and courage. Her story inspires future generations to fight for equality (Yousafzai, 2013).

.   .   .

Lessons Learned

From these stories, we learn the importance of perseverance and grit and the role of supportive communities in building resilience. These individuals show that setbacks are not failures but stepping stones toward long-term success.

Encouraging **Reflection**

- **Questions for Self-Reflection:** "What challenges have I faced that required resilience? How did I grow from these experiences?"
- **Actionable Steps:** Identify a challenge and reflect on how adopting a growth mindset could help you navigate it.

Building a Legacy of Resilience

Building a legacy of resilience is about creating lasting impacts that inspire future generations. By sharing knowledge and fostering a culture of resilience, you can contribute to the growth and strength of others.

- **Defining a Legacy of Resilience:** A legacy of resilience means leaving behind values, practices, and lessons that help others navigate life's challenges.

Steps to Building a Legacy

- **Mentoring and Guiding Others:** Share your experiences and insights with younger generations or those facing similar challenges.
- **Sharing Knowledge and Experiences:** Write, speak, or teach others about your journey and the lessons you have learned. Sharing your story can inspire others to cultivate resilience in their own lives.
- **Contributing to Resilience-Building Initiatives:** Support organizations, causes, or community initiatives that promote resilience and personal growth. Building a legacy could involve donating time, resources, or expertise to mentor others or support programs encouraging lifelong learning and adaptability.

. . .

Real-Life Examples

A Family Passing Down Resilience-Building Traditions: In many families, resilience traditions are passed down through stories, practices, and values. For example, generations of military families often teach the importance of discipline, perseverance, and adaptability in the face of change. These values, instilled from one generation to the next, build a strong legacy of resilience.

Theodore Roosevelt and the Legacy of Resilience: Theodore Roosevelt, the 26th President of the United States, is well-known for his physical and mental toughness, which he developed from a young age. As a child, Roosevelt had severe asthma and other health problems, which his father, Theodore Roosevelt Sr., addressed by encouraging him to build physical strength and embrace a strenuous, active life. Theodore Sr. often told his son, "You must make your body," pushing him to overcome his physical limitations through determination and effort (McCullough, 1981).

Theodore Roosevelt passed down this ethos of resilience, hard work, and overcoming adversity to his children, most notably to his son Kermit Roosevelt. Kermit exhibited similar traits of toughness and adaptability in the face of hardship. He became a soldier, explorer, and businessman, enduring challenges like leading expeditions to remote parts of the world and serving in two world wars. His resilience was a reflection of the lessons imparted by his father about persevering through adversity.

The Roosevelt family's emphasis on discipline, physical activity, intellectual curiosity, and courage became a tradition passed from generation to generation, fostering resilience in each family member. Theodore's example shows how resilience can be taught and instilled in future generations through deliberate effort, values, and the expectation of perseverance in the face of life's trials.

This story highlights the importance of modeling resilience and actively encouraging strength and adaptability within the family unit, helping ensure these qualities endure through generations.

．　．　．

Inspiring **Future Generations**

• **Teaching Resilience Skills to Children and Young Adults:** Educating young people about the importance of resilience and adaptability equips them with the tools they need to face life's challenges confidently. Mentorship, educational programs, and family guidance are critical in fostering future generations' resilience.

• **Creating Supportive Environments for Growth and Development:** Building environments where individuals feel safe to explore, fail, and learn fosters resilience. Whether in schools, workplaces, or communities, creating a culture that values continuous growth and learning encourages people to stretch their limits and thrive in adversity.

Biblical Example: Nehemiah's Leadership and Resilience

The story of Nehemiah in the Old Testament offers a powerful example of long-term resilience, leadership, and legacy building. Nehemiah was a Jewish official serving in the Persian court when he learned that the walls of Jerusalem had been destroyed, leaving the city vulnerable to attack. Despite the daunting task ahead, Nehemiah felt called to rebuild the walls of his ancestral city (Nehemiah 1:1–11).

Nehemiah faced significant opposition from local leaders who tried to undermine the rebuilding efforts. However, he remained steadfast, trusting in God's guidance and motivating the people of Jerusalem to keep working despite external threats. Nehemiah's resilience and determination were critical in completing the project within 52 days (Nehemiah 6:15). His leadership restored the city's physical walls and revived the spirit and faith of the Jewish people, establishing a legacy that would endure for generations.

Nehemiah's story teaches us the importance of perseverance, planning, and faith in the face of adversity. By staying committed to long-term goals and fostering a sense of community, Nehemiah built a legacy of resilience that transformed the city and its people.

. . .

REFERENCES

Blakely, S. (2018). *The story behind Spanx: How failure fueled the success of one of America's top businesswomen.* Random House.

Dweck, C. S. (2006). *Mindset: The new psychology of success.* Random House.

Gates, B. (2017). *The road ahead: Philanthropy and innovation in the 21st century.* Penguin.

Kolb, D. A. (2014). *Experiential learning: Experience as the source of learning and development.* Pearson Education.

Lazenby, R. (2014). *Michael Jordan: The life.* Little, Brown.

Locke, E. A., & Latham, G. P. (2002). Building a practically useful theory of goal setting and task motivation: A 35-year odyssey. *American Psychologist, 57*(9), 705-717.

Mandela, N. (1994). *Long walk to freedom: The autobiography of Nelson Mandela.* Little, Brown.

McCullough, D. (1981). *Mornings on horseback: The story of an extraordinary family, a vanished way of life, and the unique child who became Theodore Roosevelt.* Simon & Schuster.

Vance, A. (2015). *Elon Musk: Tesla, SpaceX, and the quest for a fantastic future.* HarperCollins.

Yousafzai, M. (2013). *I am Malala: The girl who stood up for education and was shot by the Taliban.* Little, Brown.

EPILOGUE

Conclusion: The Science and Spirit of Resilience

Resilience is more than just a skill—it is a way of life, a mindset that empowers you to face life's challenges with grace, strength, and confidence. Throughout this book, we've explored the dynamic interplay between **science** and **spirit**, uncovering how the latest findings in **neuroscience, psychology,** and **emotional health** intersect with timeless **Biblical wisdom.** Together, they provide a comprehensive framework for building resilience that can withstand adversity in all its forms.

The **science of resilience** has revealed that our brains are adaptable, our emotions manageable, and our bodies capable of transformation through straightforward, actionable practices. **Mindfulness, meditation, healthy habits,** and **positive thinking** are not just fleeting trends; they are grounded in robust research demonstrating their power to rewire our brains and improve our lives. By incorporating these strategies into your daily routine, you've taken the first steps toward becoming more resilient, not only in how you think but in how you live.

At the same time, **faith** plays an irreplaceable role in resilience. The **Biblical stories** interwoven throughout these chapters remind us that resilience is not just about personal effort. It's about trusting in something greater than ourselves. Whether we are facing personal hardships, navigating uncertainty, or striving for long-term growth, the examples of **David, Joseph, Moses**, and others show us that **faith** can carry us through the darkest times. Their stories teach us to lean on our spiritual foundations, knowing that through prayer, community, and trust in God, we find strength far beyond our own.

As you move forward, I encourage you to continue embracing the scientific practices and spiritual principles we've discussed. Take small daily steps to **practice Mindfulness, cultivate supportive relationships**, and **challenge negative thoughts**. Set **meaningful goals, track your progress**, and remember that setbacks are not the end— they are growth opportunities.

Most importantly, allow your faith to anchor you. Just as the Bible heroes we've studied drew strength from their belief in God's plan, so can you rely on your faith to provide resilience in the face of life's uncertainties. Spend time in the Word. As you grow in both **mind** and **spirit**, you will build a legacy of resilience that will transform your life and inspire and uplift those around you.

Remember, resilience is not about avoiding adversity but thriving through it. You now have the tools, knowledge, and inspiration to do just that. With science and spirit working together, your capacity for resilience is limitless.

A REQUEST

If you have found value in this book, please share your experience by leaving a rating or review on Amazon.

If you are reading an ebook, please click this link go to your review page.

If you are reading a print book, point your phone's camera at the QR code below to be taken to your review page. Thank you!

ABOUT THE AUTHOR

Elliott Middleton, PhD, is a former university professor and decision scientist at some of the world's largest financial institutions. He lives with his family in Tennessee.